*Arts of the Islamic Book*

# Arts of the Islamic Book

## THE COLLECTION OF
## PRINCE SADRUDDIN AGA KHAN

*Anthony Welch and
Stuart Cary Welch*

PUBLISHED FOR

THE ASIA SOCIETY BY

*Cornell University Press*

ITHACA AND LONDON

*Arts of the Islamic Book* is the catalogue of an exhibition organized by The Asia Society to further understanding between the peoples of the United States and Asia. The exhibition was presented in the Society's headquarters in New York City from 7 October 1982 to 2 January 1983 and then at the Kimbell Art Museum, Fort Worth, and the Nelson Gallery–Atkins Museum, Kansas City.

Preparation of the manuscript has been assisted by a grant from the Andrew W. Mellon Foundation.

Photograph credits: No. 3 by John D. Schiff; no. 30 by David Kellogg; all other photographs by Christian Poite, Geneva.

First published 1982 by Cornell University Press.
Published in the United Kingdom by Cornell University Press Ltd.,
Ely House, 37 Dover Street, London W1X 4HQ.

International Standard Book Number (cloth) 0-8014-1548-9
International Standard Book Number (paper) 0-8014-9882-1
Library of Congress Catalog Card Number 82-71587
Printed in the United States of America
*Librarians: Library of Congress cataloging information appears
on the last page of the book.*

*The paper in this book is acid-free, and meets the guidelines for permanence and durability of the Committee on Production Guidelines for Book Longevity of the Council on Library Resources.*

# Contents

# *Acknowledgments*

This book and exhibition owe their existence to Prince Sadruddin Aga Khan, who combines a connoisseur's eye, a scholar's knowledge, and a profound love for Islamic culture. The small sampling presented here of his great collection focuses on the precious manuscript and the album. Here the painter's brush and the calligrapher's pen produced what may be Islam's most personal arts—those in which we can most sharply discern the aspirations and aesthetics of their patrons.

The authors, Anthony Welch and Stuart Cary Welch, are not related, though the coincidence of surname has occasioned some confusion in scholarly circles. It was Cary Welch, at Harvard fifteen years ago, who turned Anthony Welch's eyes toward Islamic art, and who not only oversaw much of Anthony Welch's training as an art historian but also suggested that he embark on the project of publishing Prince Sadruddin's collection. Thus this present association is actually one of long standing and part of a process of collecting, teaching, and scholarship that has been under way for many years.

Authors' initials appear after each entry, but Anthony Welch wishes to note that Cary Welch's role is far more substantial than these identifications indicate. In discussion over many years, in planning and selecting the exhibition, and in intense examination of individual objects, he has been a guiding force. His well-known scholarly generosity and integrity have led him to initial only those entries that he wrote in whole or in considerable part, but to those who know his work, his greater contribution should be obvious.

Both authors are happily indebted to Prof. Dr. Annemarie Schimmel, who traveled to Geneva to see many of these selected objects and who generously shared her profound knowledge in identifying texts, naming scribes, and translating difficult passages in several languages. She also read the entire book in manuscript form, caught errors large and small, and offered many wise suggestions and improvements; without her assistance and her many contributions this would have been a different and far less worthy book.

To other scholars our debt is substantial as well, and we hope that our citation of their works in footnotes and bibliographic references will be a fitting statement of our thanks.

Through a generous 1981 study leave, the University of Victoria and the Social Sciences and Humanities Research Council of Canada have made it possible for Anthony Welch to work on this book as well as to pursue other research, and he gratefully acknowledges the assistance of both institutions.

Allen Wardwell, Director of Asia Society Gallery, and Sarah Bradley, Assistant Director, have nurtured this project from its inception and have supported it at every stage with dedication, exemplary attention to detail, and unflagging patience. It is a scholar's joy to work with them.

This collection, exhibition, and book are a testimony to a great art of a great world culture. It is fitting that this book should acknowledge a scholar who has contributed profoundly to that culture and who has immeasurably broadened our awareness of it. In friendship and with respect the authors dedicate their work here to Annemarie Schimmel.

ANTHONY WELCH
*University of Victoria*
STUART CARY WELCH
*Harvard University*

# *Foreword*

Anyone who has followed the Gallery program of The Asia Society over the past decade will recognize the name of Sadruddin Aga Khan as a frequent lender of important works to our temporary exhibitions. He has generously shared paintings and manuscripts with us on four recent occasions. They appeared, interestingly enough, in two exhibitions that were organized by Anthony Welch (*Shah ʿAbbas and the Arts of Isfahan*, 1973, and *Calligraphy in the Arts of the Muslim World*, 1979) and two exhibitions that were organized by Stuart Cary Welch (*Indian Drawings and Painted Sketches*, 1976, and *Room for Wonder: Indian Painting during the British Period*, 1978).

What we present here, therefore, builds on a well-established pattern of successful collaboration between a great private collector, two knowledgeable and talented guest curators, and an institution. It was only natural to think of organizing a whole exhibition around this one collection and to ask the Welches (who are unrelated except for their common interests and intimate knowledge of the collection) to choose the material and write about it for us.

This is not to suggest that what is shown here is simply a reassembly of previous loans, although a few works are making a return visit. The majority of these paintings and manuscripts have not been publicly exhibited. Furthermore, although a substantial part of the collection was presented in a four-volume, limited-edition catalogue that appeared between 1972 and 1978 (additional volumes are forthcoming), a good proportion of the objects in this exhibition and catalogue have not been previously published. None of the Mughal paintings were included in the earlier catalogue nor do acquisitions made by Prince Sadruddin after 1976 appear in these volumes, and it is fair to say that some of the most noteworthy objects have come into the collection in the intervening years. Even in 1971, however, Stuart Cary Welch wrote that the collection was "one of the most important in private hands." With the refinements and acquisitions that have been made in the last decade, it has grown to even greater stature, and we are pleased to present a good measure of its overall scope and quality here. In seeking to give focus to this selection, we decided to concentrate on the collection's greatest strength, the arts of the Islamic book, as represented by both the written word and the painted album leaf.

We are, of course, indebted to Prince Sadruddin for sharing these treasures with us and for all of the assistance we have received from him and his staff in the assembly, documentation, photography, and sharing of information that have been required. Both authors have cooperated fully to meet a tight schedule, and we thank Edmund Pillsbury and Emily Sano of the Kimbell Art Museum, Fort Worth, and Ralph T. Coe and Marc Wilson of the Nelson Gallery–Atkins Museum, Kansas City, for their cooperation in bringing the exhibition to their institutions. Naomi Noble Richard provided expert editorial assistance, and my own staff has performed the various tasks of editing, registrarial work, and general administration with their characteristic cheerful professionalism.

ALLEN WARDWELL
*Director*
*Asia Society Gallery*

# Introduction

Few collections are as appropriate to their owners as this remarkable group of manuscripts, miniatures, and calligraphies—a comprehensive gathering devoted to the Islamic book. They are the treasured possessions of a distinguished Muslim, Prince Sadruddin Aga Khan, whose forebears played an active role in the creation of many of these works of art.

Muslim collectors of Muslim art are few, and most of the known collections are highly specialized. Although Prince Sadruddin enjoys all art, that of Islam has long been his principal interest, and unlike most recent collectors in this field, he has not limited himself to any single medium. A visit to Prince Sadruddin's house at Bellerive reveals that the owner is a true collector, in whom discernment and enthusiasm are finely mixed. The house contains a lively assemblage of pictures, objects, and furniture of all sorts, each item related to the others because of the collector's personal and very visceral approach to art. Most of the furniture is of the sixteenth and seventeenth centuries, but the moods range from the austere to the highly dramatic. African, Eskimo, and Tibetan objects, paintings and prints by De Chirico and Munch exist harmoniously as part of a house and collection that reflect the energy and interests of their owner.

Although Prince Sadruddin and his family are well known, many who read this may be unaware of their religious and historical background. Prince Sadruddin Aga Khan is the younger son of the late Sultan Sir Mohammad Shah, who was the forty-eighth imam, or religious leader, of some twelve million Isma'ili Shi'a Muslims, a religious community that extends from the Great Wall of China to the southern tip of Africa. Shi'a Muslims trace the lineage of their imam to 'Ali, cousin and son-in-law of the Prophet. The Isma'ilis, now led by Prince Sadruddin's nephew, Prince Karim Aga Khan, separated from other Shi'a in the eighth century over a question of succession. They accepted Isma'il, eldest son of the sixth imam, as seventh imam, and were also known as the Seveners. Other Shi'a Muslims, subsequently called the Twelvers, acknowledged a younger son and his successors.

In his memoirs Prince Sadruddin's father summarized the history of the

Isma'ili sect. "Often persecuted and oppressed, the faith of my ancestors was never destroyed; at times it flourished as in the epoch of the Fatimite Caliphs, at times it was obscure and little understood. After the loss of the Fatimite Caliphate in Egypt my ancestors moved first to the highlands of Syria and the Lebanon; thence they journeyed eastwards to the mountains of Iran. They established a stronghold on the craggy peak of Alamut in the Elburz Mountains, the range which separates from the rest of Persia the provinces lying immediately to the south of the Caspian. . . .

"In this period, the Ismaili faith was well known in Syria, in Iraq, in Arabia itself, and far up into Central Asia. Cities such as Samarkand and Bokhara were then great centres of Muslim learning and thought. A little later in the thirteenth century of the Christian era, Ismaili religious propaganda penetrated into what is now Sinkiang and Chinese Turkestan. There was a time in the thirteenth and fourteenth centuries when the Ismaili doctrine was the chief and most influential school of thought; but later, with the triumph of the Safavi Dynasty in Iran (particularly in the northwest province, Azerbaijan), the Isna Ashari, or Twelfth Imam, sect established its predominance. Remnants of the Ismaili faith remained firm and are still to be found in many parts of Asia, North Africa, and Iran. The historical centres of Ismailism indeed are scattered widely over the Islamic world" (*The Memoirs of Aga Khan* [London: Cassell and Company, 1954], p. 180).

Prince Sadruddin's great-grandfather, the first to be known as the Aga Khan, was the hereditary chieftain of the Iranian city of Kerman and the son-in-law of the Qajar ruler Fath 'Ali Shah (see cat. no. 44), as well as the imam of the Isma'ilis. In 1838, however, a question of family honor embroiled the Aga Khan in a fierce conflict with the prime minister and favorite of the shah. After several military encounters the Aga Khan, attended by his horsemen, was forced to leave Persia through the deserts of Baluchistan and Sind. During the early 1840s he and his cavalry served the British cause in Afghanistan, Sind, and the Panjab. In 1845 he reached Bombay, where he was warmly received by the Khoja Muslim community. A few years later he established his *durkhana,* or headquarters, there; and it was in Bombay that his grandson, Prince Sadruddin's father, spent his childhood.

In the third Aga Khan, East met West. Succeeding his father as imam of the Isma'ilis in 1885 when he was seven years old, he received both an Islamic and a Western education. A dedicated leader of his own community, he became an important voice for India's Muslims as a whole. He was received by Queen Victoria in 1898 and joined Lord Curzon's Indian Legislative Council as its youngest member in 1902. From 1906 to 1912 he presided over the All-India Muslim League, and in 1937 he became president of the League of Nations. The Aga Khan died in 1957 and was succeeded as imam by his grandson, Prince Karim.

In a tribute to his father at the centenary of his birth, Prince Sadruddin wrote of him for the London *Times:* "My father was first and foremost a deeply religious man who had no difficulty in integrating an active political and social life and everything it entailed in terms of formality and obligations in the post-Victorian era, with the close communion with God which is the aspiration of every practicing Muslim" (*The Times*, 5 November 1977).

The family tradition of leadership and public service is clearly evident in Prince Sadruddin's own life. Inasmuch as his father presided over the League of Nations, it seems appropriate that he has served the United Nations for many years. He became a UNESCO Consultant for Afro-Asian Projects in 1958, four years after he had taken his degree in government at Harvard University and done graduate work at Harvard's Center for Middle Eastern Studies. The following year he was appointed Head of Mission and Adviser to the U.N. High Commissioner for Refugees, a post he held for two years. In 1961 he served as Special Consultant to the Director-General and as Executive Secretary to the UNESCO International Action Committee for the Preservation of Nubian Monuments. From 1962 until 1965 he was U.N. Deputy High Commissioner for Refugees, and from 1965 until 1977 he served as High Commissioner for Refugees. Since then he has been a Special Consultant and Chargé de Mission to the Secretary-General of the United Nations; and recently he was very nearly elected U.N. Secretary-General.

Prince Sadruddin has been awarded many decorations and distinctions, including the U.N. Human Rights Award and the Dag Hammarskjold Honorary Medal. He serves as president of the Council on Islamic Affairs in New York City, and he is the founder of the Bellerive Foundation as well as founder and president of the Groupe de Bellerive, an organization bringing together physicists, philosophers, university professors, jurists, politicians, and churchmen who address themselves periodically to problems related to science and society. To date their work has focussed essentially on nuclear technology and the proliferation of armaments. For many years Prince Sadruddin has also been publisher of *The Paris Review*. It is not, however, the honors and achievements of his public life that concern us here; it is his private avocation. The collection of Islamic art begun modestly when he was a student at Harvard and enlivened by careful additions and deletions over the past thirty years is now one of the most important in private hands.

Happily the early 1950s were auspicious years for collectors of Islamic art. In New York City several art dealers possessed inherited collections of outstanding miniatures, calligraphies, ceramics, and other objects. A visit to Adrienne Minassian's storeroom in a warehouse on 55th Street was always a rich and rewarding experience. Two large steel cabinets contained stacks of black portfolios, each bursting with Timurid, Ottoman, Safavid, and Mughal drawings and miniatures, while as many others contained folios from Qur'ans and other manuscripts in every sort of script, from Kufic to Shikastah. Magnificent pages from albums assembled and illuminated for Shah Jahan were cheek by jowl with Qajar *firmans* and Safavid miniatures. Other cabinets were devoted to pottery and metalwork. Timurid, Safavid, and Ottoman dishes glazed in deep greens and blues were stacked in such quantity that it required several hours of hard looking—usually while standing high on a chair—to see them. Beneath a large Jacobean refectory table, architectural fragments, including a beautiful bit of stucco from the Alhambra, added a further rich note to the scene, which we always recall with delight: a collector's dream, along with an admixture of Ye Olde Curiosity Shoppe.

During his years as an undergraduate and graduate student at Harvard, Prince Sadruddin made frequent excursions to New York, and on those occasions visits to Miss Minassian were unscheduled but regular events. Although we never accompanied the prince, we envision busy, rather dusty (and in winter very cold) scenes in which he educated his eye by rummaging through the wonders of Miss Minassian's 55th Street treasure house. One such visit was rewarded by one of the most splendid pages from the 1354 *Automata* manuscript (cat. no. 3), in which large areas of tarnished silver and gold draw one's eye to the intricacies of a Mamluk medical fantasy. We had long enjoyed other powerful pictures from this book in the Islamic galleries of the Boston Museum of Fine Arts, and it was a still greater pleasure to study a superb page that belonged to a friend. Another quarry from these early days of hunting is a lively, early fifteenth-century drawing, probably from Tabriz, showing a lion threatening two monkeys, who in turn taunt him maddeningly (cat. no. 15). Very likely it originally came from one of the albums, now in Istanbul and Berlin, that must once have belonged to the great royal library of Tabriz, a library that passed successively from Mongol to Jala'irid, Timurid, Turcoman, and Safavid rulers. This sprightly drawing, along with another of slightly later date depicting a hero killing a dragon in a fervidly animated wood (cat. no. 14), is one of the few removed from the royal albums. And it seems especially fortunate that these two important and beautiful pictures, which must have been studied and appreciated by a long line of Iranian and Turkish princes and artists, should have found their home in a Muslim collection.

Another productive source of Islamic objects in New York was H. Khan Monif, the son of an Iranian general. He had come to New York by way of Paris in the 1930s and had brought with him a generous sampling of Iranian art: Luristan and Islamic bronzes, glass, pottery, and miniatures. A merchant of the old school, he priced objects according to their cost to him, adding invariably the same margin of profit. As a result, objects of aesthetic merit cost no more than those of mere historical interest, a circumstance which encouraged connoisseurship. Such dealers as Miss Minassian and Mr. and Mrs. Nasli Heeramaneck were fully aware of levels of quality, but Mr. Monif chose to ignore such factors. Accordingly, Prince Sadruddin and several other collectors of the early 1950s made productive forays into the always changing stock of the Monif store. When the rumor of a shipment spread abroad, collectors vied with one another for the first look. The better objects were not likely to linger in Mr. Monif's hands for more than a few hours. A number of the prince's visits there resulted in the purchase of excellent miniatures and fourteenth-century bronze candlesticks; other occasions were "educational." The dealer loved to reminisce about the troubled days in Iran that his father and he had seen. The old general had watched magnificent textiles burned to melt out the gold threads. And Khan Monif himself told of the day in Paris when he had been offered the great Il-Khanid *Shahnamah,* now known as the "Demotte *Shahnamah,*" after the dealer who eventually acquired it and sold its pages separately. But at that time Khan Monif had turned the masterpiece down, feeling that its quality did not warrant its "excessive" price (a price that was, in fact, a fraction of what a single page would bring today).

One of this dealer's most helpful contributions to his visitors' artistic enlightenment was his knowledge of forgeries and retouching. Restorations of pottery objects, as well as repainted faces in miniatures, were always pointed out scrupulously, sometimes to the accompaniment of tales, recounted with ominous glee, of rival specialists' shortcomings in this respect. Of particular interest was the story of the opium addict in Paris who was able to separate versos and rectos of a single folio by masterful tearing. He could also repaint damaged pictures or create outright forgeries with a skill that could dupe all but the keenest experts.

After graduate school Prince Sadruddin spent more time in Europe. He also traveled more extensively; and whenever the opportunity presented itself, he gave up as much time as he could from his work for the United Nations to visit and study other collections and to add to his own. With increasing eagerness he bought from the dealers in London, Paris, and Switzerland, as well as from the auction houses. As he gained in experience, so did the collection gain in quality; and as time passed, opportunities for acquisition multiplied. Worldwide interest in Islamic art had quickened. There were more and better auctions. Sales catalogues, formerly skimpy, ill researched, and ungenerously illustrated, fattened; and before long they contained not only a plethora of black-and-white illustrations but color plates as well. Specialized dealerships mushroomed in Paris, London, and New York; and august establishments on Bond Street, long noted for their Old Master and Impressionist pictures, soon developed expertise in the mysteries of the East. The fascinating clutter of antiquarians' storage rooms, where collectors enjoyed the adventure of sifting through accumulations of good, bad, and indifferent material, gave way to immaculate galleries, where a few spotlighted miniatures or objects were shown far more enticingly. Ye Olde Curiosity Shoppe had been replaced by stage sets. And of course this sophisticated ambience brought with it a more urbane and suave cast of characters. It also unearthed many works of art. Grand old collections, formed in the days of the Turkish Corner and lovingly protected by their inheritors as styles changed from art nouveau to deco to Bauhaus and eventually—full circle—back to oriental exoticism, emerged from their repositories. Louis J. Cartier's splendid miniatures and manuscripts were sold in the 1950s. Other troves followed. A culmination of these artistic changes of hand took place on Old Bond Street in April 1976, when miniatures and manuscripts brought together by generations of Rothschilds, together with more recently gathered material from Edwin Binney, 3rd, were sold through Colnaghi's. Museum curators and private collectors the world over seized this opportunity to acquire superb works of art of a sort—and in a quantity—not likely to be offered again. On this occasion Prince Sadruddin acquired a number of magnificent pictures, including several folios from Shah Isma'il II's *Shahnamah*, often thought to be the last "great" Safavid version of the epic (cat. no. 29). At this time he also bought remarkable Indian miniatures: the *Genealogy of Emperor Jahangir* (cat. no. 70), *An Aged Pilgrim* by Abu'l-Hasan, Jahangir's favorite painter (cat. no. 68), Bishndas's *Portrait of Shah 'Abbas I* (cat. no. 67), and Muhammad 'Ali's *Noble Hunt* (cat. no. 65). Further brilliant acquisitions were made when another ex-Rothschild manuscript was dismantled and a number of its miniatures sold. The Houghton *Shahnamah*, commissioned by Shah Tahmasp Safavi, now named after Arthur A. Houghton, Jr., its last owner, was the source of Prince Sadruddin's *The Story of Haftwad and the Worm*, signed by Master Dust Muhammad, and of Aqa Mirak's *Firdausi Encounters the Court Poets of Ghazna*, which contains a portrait of the youthful patron himself (cat. no. 22[A]).

One could cite extraordinary miniatures and calligraphies from Prince Sadruddin's collection endlessly; but it is far more instructive and pleasurable to turn to the material itself, as represented here. For this sampling of the collection is certain to delight and instruct. It also provides insights into the personality of the collector, particularly his deep concern for people of all sorts and ages—a characteristic also expressed in his devotion to the cause of refugees. Although Prince Sadruddin's collection has been secondary to his humanitarianism, the gusto, sympathy, and joyous sense of humor so evident in the pictures are the very qualities that have made his many years of public service so effective.

STUART CARY WELCH

*Arts of the Islamic Book*

# The Arab Lands

The revelation of the Holy Qur'an to the Prophet Muhammad between A.D. 610 and 632 transformed Arabia into the heartland of a great world faith. It was also the impetus for the subsequent rapid expansion of the Arab people. They took with them Islam, the Qur'an, the Arabic language, and the Arabic script, all essential to the creation of Islamic culture. Due to the preeminence of the Qur'an in Muslim life, calligraphy has always been considered the highest form of art. The *qalam,* or reed pen, is said to have been the first of God's creations, and the Prophet's cousin and son-in-law ʿAli the first calligrapher. In most periods the scribe therefore occupied a more exalted position than the painter, whose figural art, due to orthodox strictures against "graven images," was almost entirely restricted to expressions of secular culture. It was the scribe who could perform the most pious of arts, the copying of God's words.

The earliest known illustrated Arabic manuscript is an astronomical text dating to A.D. 1009. Although classics of Arabic literature, such as the *Kalila wa Dimna* animal fables and the *Maqamat* of Hariri, were widely copied and illustrated in the thirteenth and fourteenth centuries in Mesopotamia and Egypt, the illustration of scientific and quasi-scientific texts, such as al-Jazari's *Book of Knowledge of Ingenious Mechanical Devices,* continued to be a major function of Arab painters.

Techniques developed in this period remained basic for most later Islamic painting. Gouache on paper, widely used in Islam after the middle of the ninth century, was the general medium, and the brush, usually made from the hair of a cat or a squirrel, was the instrument of application. Paintings, like calligraphies, were almost always parts of larger works, either manuscripts of literary works or precious albums in which specimens of script, illumination, and figural paintings were brought together in a harmonious whole. The production of a Muslim manuscript or album was a collective effort, involving other artists besides calligraphers and painters: paper-makers, gilders, illuminators, and binders were essential to the production of a book. Thus a royal library was not simply a repository of books but was also often a workshop where diverse talents under one direction collaborated in the creation of one of Islam's most refined arts.

## 1 / Page from a Qur'an
North Africa; late 9th or early 10th century
H. 28.6 cm., W. 35 cm.

This page comes from a Qur'an that was one of the most sumptuous creations of medieval Islam. Written in a gold Kufic style of script on blue vellum, its oblong horizontal format is characteristic of early Qur'ans, as is the lack of diacritical marks, and though their absence might diminish legibility, it enhances grace. The page's fifteen lines accentuate this book's shape: verticality is limited, and repeated words and letters can both be of varying lengths—some very compact, others vastly extended—to emphasize textual importance and to set up a tightly controlled composition based not on legibility but on aesthetic structure. Thus, many words are broken, with an initial letter at the end of one line and the remainder on the next. The blue and gold color scheme is apparently unique, and though the Arabic script moves from right to left, the pages of this Qur'an—unlike almost all others—were turned from left to right, the left-hand page preceding the right.[1]

The text comes from *surah al-Baqarah,* 2:148–50:

> . . . [so vie with one another] in good works. Wheresoever ye may be, Allah will bring you all together. Lo! Allah is Able to do all things.
>
> And whencesoever thou comest forth (for prayer, O Muhammad) turn thy face toward the Inviolable Place of Worship. Lo! it is the Truth from thy Lord. Allah is not unaware of what ye do.
>
> Whencesoever thou comest forth turn thy face toward the Inviolable Place of Worship; and wheresoever ye may be (O Muslims) turn your faces toward it (when ye pray) so that men may have no argument against you, save such as them as do injustice—Fear them not, but fear Me!—and so that I may complete My grace upon you, and that ye may be guided.[2]

Its sumptuousness and rarity make it unlikely that this manuscript of Islam's central scripture was anything other than a royal production, made either for a caliph or as a caliphal donation to a major religious center. Although there is some scholarly debate about the manuscript's origins,[3] it seems most likely that it was produced on caliphal order in Kairouan—the great religious, social, and cultural center of medieval North Africa—for the Great Mosque there.

A.W.

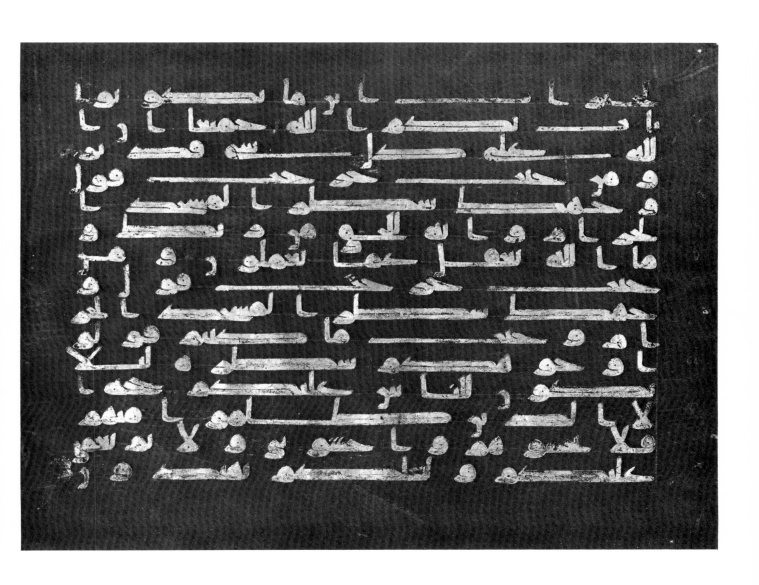

1 / (also in color)

1. The original manuscript in almost complete condition is in the Museum of Islamic Art, National Institute of Archaeology and Arts, Tunis. In publishing two folios from it, Martin Lings and Yasin H. Safadi (*The Qur'an* [London, 1976], p. 25 [no. 11]) mention this "reverse" pagination. Other pages from this manuscript are in the Fogg Art Museum, Cambridge, Massachusetts; the Museum of Fine Arts, Boston; and the Chester Beatty Library, Dublin.

2. This and all subsequent translations from the Qur'an are from *The Glorious Koran*, a bilingual edition with English translation, introduction, and notes by Marmaduke Pickthall (London, 1976).

3. Two opposing arguments have been offered to explain the book's provenance. The first is based on a statement of Frederick R. Martin, who makes the earliest reference in Western scholarly literature to the manuscript: "I have quite recently acquired leaves from the *Koran* which was written on blue vellum by order of the caliph al-Ma'mun for the tomb of his father, Harun al-Rashid, at Mashhad . . ." (*The Miniature Paintings and Painters of Persia, India, and Turkey* [London, 1912], p. 141). Martin cites no evidence for this attribution, which seems to form the basis for a more recent argument that the book was produced in Baghdad (Christie's catalogue, *Khurasan*, London, 9 November 1977). The second argument has been put forward by Lings and Safadi, *The Qur'an*, who mention no colophon for the manuscript and who provide substantial evidence that this book, like a great many other early Kufic Qur'ans, was produced in Kairouan. (See also Anthony Welch, *Calligraphy in the Arts of the Muslim World* [Austin and London, 1979], pp. 48–49.) Stylistic similarity between the script in this Qur'an and contemporary calligraphy from the region of Baghdad, the 'Abbasid capital, is not a determinative point, since court styles in art were widely disseminated throughout the caliphate.

PUBLISHED: Alexandra Raeuber, *Islamische Schönschrift* (Zürich: Rietberg Museum, 1979), fig. 5.

## 2 / Page from a Qur'an
North Africa; 13th–14th century
H. 25.4 cm., W. 17.8 cm.

Maghribi script style was limited to North Africa and Spain, and scribes from Egypt eastward viewed it as uncanonical, for its principal formative module was the whole word rather than the component letters. Its horizontal emphasis and its idiosyncratic tendencies derive from an earlier Kufic mode, but its major trait is the swooping, irregularly rounded arcs, balanced by other elements that bend and curve and double back to give a weighty stateliness to the text.[1]

On each side of this light brown parchment page are nine lines written in gold in Maghribi. Red and blue diacritical marks aid the reader, and gold roundels, with the word *aya* (verse) written in white on blue inside them, mark the end of each verse.

The text comes from the Qur'an's *surah Bani Isra'il* (*Children of Israel*) 17:75–79:

> . . . [then] hadst thou found no helper against Us.
> And they indeed wish to scare thee from the land that they might drive thee forth from thence, and then they would have stayed (there) but a little after thee.

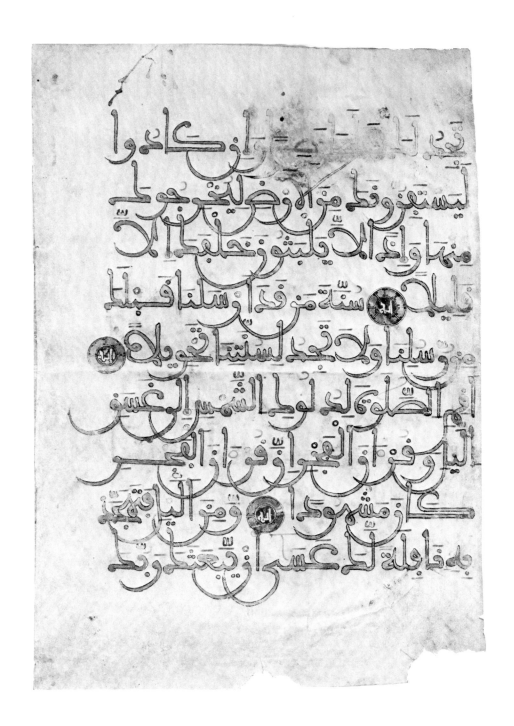

(Such was Our) method in the case of those whom We sent before thee (to mankind), and thou wilt not find for Our method aught of power to change.

Establish worship at the going down of the sun until the dark of night, and (the recital of) the Qur'an at dawn. Lo! (the recital of) the Qur'an at dawn is ever witnessed.

And some part of the night awake for it, a largess for thee. It may be that thy Lord will raise thee [to a praised estate].

The preceding four verses of the *surah* are on the other side.

A. W.

1. For additional information on the Maghribi style, see Anthony Welch, *Calligraphy in the Arts of the Muslim World* (Austin and London, 1979), pp. 70–71.

PUBLISHED: Alexandra Raeuber, *Islamische Schönschrift* (Zürich: Rietberg Museum, 1979), fig. 19; Anthony Welch, *Collection of Islamic Art, Prince Sadruddin Aga Khan,* 4 vols. (Geneva, 1972–78), vol. 2, Cal. 3. All four volumes of this work are referred to hereafter as *Collection.*

## 3 / A Blood-Measuring Device
Egypt; February–March 1354
From a manuscript of al-Jazari's *Automata*
Page: H. 39.1 cm., W. 27.4 cm.

About 1206 the inventor and scholar Badi al-Zaman ibn al-Razzaz al-Jazari completed an Arabic treatise entitled *Kitab fi Ma'rifat al-Hiyal al-Hand-asiya,* or *Book of Knowledge of Ingenious Mechanical Devices.*[1] The book, more generally known as al-Jazari's *Automata,* was designed to satisfy the interest of the Artuqid sultan of Diyarbakir (in modern Turkey) in mechanical gadgetry. The fifty devices that al-Jazari invented, explicated, and had illustrated for Sultan Nasir al-Din Muhammad (r. 1201–1222) may have been constructable, even constructed, or they may have been wholly imaginary; there is, unfortunately, no extant example of one of his automata. In any case, his work reflects a fascination with elaborate machinery that was characteristic of medieval culture in the eastern Mediterranean and the Middle East. Al-Jazari's book was popular and widely copied.[2] The Egyptian manuscript of 1354 from which this illustrated page comes was written not for the reigning Mamluk sultan Hasan but for one of his prominent amirs, Nasir al-Din Muhammad ibn Tulak al-Hasani al-Malik al-Salih. The text and fourteen original illustrations from this finest of extant *Automata* manuscripts are preserved in Istanbul;[3] the rest of the original illustrations are widely dispersed. The scribe, Muhammad ibn Ahmad al-Izmiri, was a competent practitioner of *naskh* and *thuluth,* and the inscription at the top of this page reads: "This is a device in the shape of a basin. It is a basin, and a cubus, and cylinders."

The book is divided into six parts, and this painting illustrates chapter 7 of part 3, which was devoted to machines to assist in blood-letting and ablutions. The instrument was designed to operate with wonderful redundancy. As the liquid was collected in the basin, the several weights and pulleys manipulated the three figures seated on the platform: the small man at the left noted on his slate each *dirham* of fluid; the man at the right indicated the same number of *dirhams* with his pointer on a circle laid out horizontally in front of him; in front of the large middle figure is a disk to which are attached ten hands, each in a distinct gesture, and at every tenth *dirham* the disk rotated to indicate the new fluid level. Obviously this was not a purely utilitarian design, and the element of humor in all these models may well have been intentional.

Like much Mamluk painting, this work is stylistically closely related to earlier art from Syria and Iraq. Much of the artistic talent of the Middle East had emigrated to Mamluk Egypt after the Mongol conquest, and Mamluk sultans and amirs were justly celebrated as lavish patrons of the arts of architecture, metalwork, and the precious manuscript.

A. W.

1. For further bibliography and discussion of al-Jazari's *Automata*, see Donald Hill, *The Book of Knowledge of Ingenious Mechanical Devices* (Dordrecht and Boston, 1974); and Esin Atil, *Art of the Arab World* (Washington, D.C., 1975), pp. 102–11. Atil's entry no. 52 deals specifically with the 1354 Mamluk manuscript. The first extant manuscript of the *Automata* was copied from al-Jazari's holograph text and was completed in 1206; it contains sixty illustrations, presumably also based on al-Jazari's own work.

2. Fourteen copies are extant (see Atil, *Art of the Arab World*, p. 149, n. 12). Their illustrations are ultimately based on the 1206 manuscript; faithful copying of illustrations is characteristic of medieval Muslim scientific treatises.

3. Süleymaniye Library (Aya Sofya, no. 3606). The colophon, fortunately preserved, recounts the creation of the manuscript.

PUBLISHED: Ernst Blochet, *Musulman Painting* (London, 1929), pl. 36; Anthony Welch, *Collection*, vol. 1, A. M. 3.

# Ottoman Turkey

Although Turkish-speaking peoples had progressively settled the Anatolian peninsula from the eleventh century, the key event for the Turkish art of the book was the rise of the Ottoman state and its conquest of Constantinople in 1453. This marked the beginning of the most active and creative period of Ottoman patronage, when the vast resources of an immense and diverse empire could be turned to architecture and the arts. Ottoman sultans could attract talent from all over the Muslim world, particularly Iran, but Ottoman art rapidly developed its own distinctive aesthetics and dynamic. Some of Islam's finest calligraphers worked under Ottoman patronage and founded schools and styles that endured for many generations. The illustration of epic poetry and the Ottomans' own epic history became major tasks for court painters, and a brilliant art of portraiture developed that serves as a dynastic record of the rulers and their key officials. The Ottomans were equally fascinated with the content of their vast state—its geography, history, structure, peoples, and social strata, and as in Mughal India, painters delineated the expansion of the empire and the forms of its myriad elements with an exactitude that delights historians of society as well as art.

## 4 / A Manuscript of the Qur'an
Turkey; ca. 1500–1510
H. 38.8 cm., W. 26.3 cm.

Calligraphers, like painters, prided themselves on their artistic descent, and the great early Ottoman scribe, Shaykh Hamdallah ibn Mustafa, claimed descent from the line of Yaqut, the mid-thirteenth-century master who had developed the six traditional styles of writing to what was widely

regarded as perfection. Calligraphers measured their art against Yaqut's standards. Shaykh Hamdallah was born in the eastern Turkish city of Amasya in 1439 or 1440, and there gained such a reputation that he instructed the Ottoman prince Bayazid, who was governor of Amasya until 1481. When Bayazid became sultan, Shaykh Hamdallah moved with him to Istanbul, where he was honored with the same lofty epithet that Yaqut had enjoyed, "*qiblah*[1] of the calligraphers," and where he must have been director of the imperial library. He enjoyed enormous favor and high salary and during the next three decades is said to have completed forty-six entire Qur'ans and a thousand sections of the scripture. He was also an active and apparently gifted teacher, training not only his own close relations but also many well-known scribes who perpetuated his styles as he had perpetuated Yaqut's. The high point of his career coincides with the reign of Sultan Bayazid II (1481–1512), and he remained an intimate companion of that often beleaguered ruler throughout his reign. He lived on until 1519, and despite his close association with Bayazid, he probably also served under his fractious son and successor, Selim the Grim (r. 1512–1520).

This magnificent Qur'an's colophon unfortunately provides neither date nor name of patron, but it does identify the copyist as "Shaykh Hamdallah ibn Mustafa, the perfect hajji[2] and the head of the scribes." Most of the book's 278 pages are written in 13 lines of superbly measured *naskh* enclosed in simple gold-and-blue borders, but *surah* headings indicate that a master illuminator was Shaykh Hamdallah's collaborator. Their finest joint achievement is, appropriately, the book's opening pages (illustrated), presenting the Qur'an's initial *surah* and the first verses of its second. Since the manuscript is of the highest quality and its colophon identifies the calligrapher as "head of the scribes," it is an altogether reasonable assumption that this Qur'an, one of a very few extant early Ottoman royal Qur'ans, was made for Bayazid, probably in the last decade of his turbulent reign. Plagued by feuding sons and many wars, the aging sultan must have found a measure of calm in the harmony and clarity of the illuminator's ordered relationships and in the balance and restrained elegance of Shaykh Hamdallah's *naskh*.

A. W.

1. *Qiblah* is a term identifying the direction of Mecca and, hence, the prayer wall of a mosque. The "*qiblah* of calligraphers" would have been the acknowledged master, one whose work was looked on as a model by all other scribes.
2. A hajji is a Muslim who has completed the pilgrimage to Mecca and Medina.

PUBLISHED: Anthony Welch, *Collection,* vol. 2, no. 5; Martin Lings and Yasin H. Safadi, *The Qur'an* (London, 1976), no. 129; Anthony Welch, *Calligraphy in the Arts of the Muslim World* (Austin and London, 1979), no. 29.

## 5 / Young Falconer

Attrib. to Wali Jan
Turkey; second half 16th century
Page: H. 11.9 cm., W. 5.9 cm.
Miniature: H. 10.2 cm., W. 3.2 cm.

The *simurgh* (a phoenix-like mythical bird) trailing long feathers in the sky is usually a symbol of mystical awareness. Here, however, the myth's other side is shown, and the giant bird is at least rapacious, if not actually malevolent. The small birds are more frightened of it than they are of the falcon nonchalantly perched on the young man's hand. The youth seems no heavier than the falcon: he balances weightlessly on the tip of one boot as the tree curves around his courtly form and caressingly supports him. The elegant falcon hunt in a springtime setting is a common theme in Islamic art,[1] and the idling, beautiful youth is an even more common image in sixteenth-century Iranian culture.

Sixteenth-century Ottoman drawings, of which this is a superb example, are far less well known than historical miniatures. The present example invites an attribution to Shah Quli, a Tabriz contemporary of the great Safavid master Sultan Muhammad. He went to Rum (Turkey) in the early sixteenth century and in time became the director of the "House of Painting" of Sultan Sulayman the Magnificent (r. 1520–1566). A drawing of a playful dragon is in the album made for Bahram Mirza in the Topkapi Palace Museum, and it bears an attribution to him in the knowledgeable hand of Master Dust Muhammad, who prepared the album for Shah Tahmasp's brother.[2] Unfortunately the dragon's spirited, bold line differs considerably from the finer, harder, and less spontaneous handling of the present work, which more closely resembles signed and inscribed pictures by Shah Quli's follower, Wali Jan, to whom we must tentatively assign it.[3]

S. C. W. and A. W.

1. See cat. no. 56.

2. For information about Shah Quli, see Martin B. Dickson and Stuart C. Welch, *The Houghton Shahnameh* (Cambridge, Mass., 1981), 1:9, 54, 244 n. 14, 246 n. 6. Several other drawings have been ascribed to Shah Quli (see Laurence Binyon, J. V. S. Wilkinson, and Basil Gray, *Persian Miniature Painting* [London, 1933], pp. 107, 118, 135–36; and Esin Atil, ed., *Turkish Art* [Washington, D. C., 1980], no. 89), but his artistic development remains uncertain.

3. For two closely related drawings, see P. W. Schulz, *Die persisch-islamische Miniaturmalerei* (Leipzig, 1914), vol. 2, pl. 146 (middle and left).

PUBLISHED: Anthony Welch, *Collection*, vol. 3, Ir. M. 66.

5 /

**6** / Portrait of Sultan Selim II
By Ra'is Haydar
Turkey, Istanbul; ca. 1570
Page: H. 44.1 cm., W. 31.2 cm.
Miniature: H. 37.4 cm., W. 24.5 cm.

The long reign of Sultan Sulayman the Magnificent (r. 1520–1566) had seen the Ottoman empire reach the apogee of its power and prestige in Europe and the Muslim world, and his successor, Selim II (r. 1566–1574), inherited at the age of forty-two a state possessed of enormous wealth and a superb administrative apparatus. There was relative peace in Europe and Asia, and though the Ottomans were briefly set back by the naval defeat at Lepanto, their domination of the Mediterranean continued. Selim II was neither a *ghazi* (fighter for Islam) nor an administrator, and he left details of governance to his capable *vazir* Mehmet Sokullu. The sultan's inordinate fondness for wine earned him the epithet Selim the Sot, but he was a competent poet and a discerning patron. Under his aegis the crowning achievement of Ottoman architecture—the Selimiye Mosque in Edirne—was built by the empire's greatest architect, Sinan, and literature, music, calligraphy, and the other arts flourished at the court in Istanbul.

About midway in his eight-year reign the sultan posed for this portrait in the Topkapi Palace. An attendant wearing a green outer garment and a brilliant red hat stands behind him, and a servant, also in green, is barely visible in the arched doorway at the far left. Justifying his nickname, the corpulent sultan holds a cup of wine in his left hand, and his expression indicates that he has already been drinking. His brilliant scarlet coat is striped with short, wavy, dark red lines. In the upper left niche in the painting is written a talismanic formula against bookworms: *"Ya kabikach."* It was probably added in the late sixteenth century, when the portrait was bound in an album.[1]

In the Islamic empires of the fifteenth, sixteenth, and seventeenth centuries, princes and high officials and officers were commonly amateur artists as well as patrons. The best-known painter under Selim II, particularly famed for his portraiture, was a former naval captain, Ra'is Haydar, known as Nigari, who had become director of the imperial shipyards in Istanbul.[2] He executed a powerful portrait of the great admiral Khayr al-Din Barbarossa, wearing a similar striped red garment, before the commander's death in 1546.[3] On stylistic grounds this painting of Selim II is firmly attributable to him and must be ranked as one of the superb achievements of Ottoman portraiture.[4]

A. W.

**6** / (also in color)

1. On the reverse is an illustration originally made in Qazvin, Iran, ca. 1590, for a copy of Jami's *Khiradnamah-i Iskandar* or Nizami's *Iskandarnamah*. Our thanks to Annemarie Schimmel for identifying the talismanic invocation and the text on the reverse.

2. This information, summarized from the chronicle of the Ottoman man of letters Mustafa 'Ali, is presented in Ivan Stchoukine, *La Peinture turque d'après les manuscrits illustrés*, part 1 (Paris, 1966), pp. 29–30.

3. See Nurhan Atasoy and Filiz Çagman, *Turkish Miniature Painting* (Istanbul, 1974), pl. 20.

4. Stchoukine, *La Peinture turque*, reproduces in pls. 27 and 30 two group portraits including the sultan, from the 1568–1569 *Nuzhet al-Akhbar der Sefer-e Sigetvar* and from the ca. 1570 *Shahnamah-i Selim Khan*. Edwin Binney, 3rd, *Turkish Treasures* (Portland, Ore., 1979), no. 40b, publishes a posthumous portrait of the sultan.

## 7 / The Ottoman Army Marches on Tunis

By 'Ali
Turkey, Istanbul; 1581
From the *Shahnamah-i Selim Khan*, folio 65a
Page: H. 32.9 cm., W. 21.9 cm.
Miniature: H. 26.9 cm., W. 18.8 cm.

Ottoman rulers were keenly interested in detailed histories of their reigns, and as in sixteenth-century Mughal India, the illustration of historical works was a major occupation for court painters. Loqman was the most highly regarded of Ottoman historians and had already written a number of royal historical works when he was commissioned by Sultan Selim II[1] (r. 1566–1574) to compose a chronicle of his reign. Completed in 1581 during the reign of Sultan Murad III (1574–1595), the *Shahnamah-i Selim Khan* was modeled on the verse of Firdausi's epic *Shahnamah*.[2] The book's introduction contains valuable information on Ottoman historiography as well as on the strict superintendence hedging the author: despite his established reputation, Loqman had to submit samples of his writing and his prospectus for the text to Sultan Selim and to the chief Ottoman religious authority, and the scribe and painters had to obtain similar royal approval before the project could begin.

The largest part of the *Shahnamah-i Selim Khan* is preserved in Istanbul, but a number of pages are dispersed in several public and private collections. This page was originally folio 65a of the manuscript.

A great strategic and commercial center for North Africa, Tunis had first come under direct Ottoman suzerainty in 1534 but had been only briefly held, for the Ottomans' western rival, Hapsburg Spain, gained effective control of the city in the following year. In 1569 a powerful Ottoman army under General 'Uluj 'Ali marched west and retook the city, and it is this march toward Tunis that is illustrated here.

Two master painters provided the miniatures. The senior of them, Osman, can be considered the finest and most innovative of Ottoman histor-

7 /

ical painters; working with him was his brother-in-law ʿAli, who painted in a closely similar style and was responsible for this page. In general, Ottoman painting centered on histories, portraits, and scenes of official life and, as a result, early developed a penchant for historical and geographic accuracy and a predilection for factual reporting and straightforward, uncomplicated naturalism.

A. W.

1. Selim II is portrayed in cat. no. 6.

2. Though unfortunately no longer complete, the *Shahnamah-i Selim Khan* is preserved in the Topkapi Palace Museum, Ms. III A 3545. For an analysis of the manuscript and its place in the history of Ottoman art, see Filiz Ögütmen-Çagman, "Sehname-i Selim Han ve Minyatürleri," *Sanat Tarihi Yilligi*, no. 5, Istanbul, 1973, pp. 411–42; and Nurhan Atasoy and Filiz Çagman, *Turkish Miniature Painting* (Istanbul, 1974), pp. 34–36. I am indebted to Nurhan Atasoy for identifying this page as folio 65a of the *Shahnamah-i Selim Khan*.

PUBLISHED: Anthony Welch, Collection, vol. 3, T. M. 1.

## 8 / An Ottoman Official

Turkey; ca. 1650
Page: H. 29 cm., W. 17.9 cm.
Miniature: H. 22.3 cm., W. 13 cm.

This is a person of substance. His brown robe is lined with white fur, and his lavender turban is huge. His feet are barely visible beneath his voluminous robes, and the book in his left arm indicates that he is a man of learning. Though he is unidentified on the miniature, he must have been an official of importance, for he stands under a golden arch, and everything about him indicates wealth and position.

This portrait was once mounted in an album. On its reverse is a page from Saʿdi's *Gulistan*. Although most of the text is badly effaced, a few lines of legible poetry identify it as story 31 from part 2:

A man, being tormented by a contrary wind in his belly and not having the power to retain it, unwittingly allowed it to escape. He said: "Friends, I had no option in what I did, the fault of it is not to be ascribed to me and peace has resulted to my internal parts. Kindly excuse me."

The belly is a prison of wind, O wise man.
No sage retains wind in captivity.
If wind twists thy belly let it out,
Because wind in the belly is a burden
    to the heart. [1]

The witty story presumably had no bearing on the individual portrayed here.

A. W.

1. Edward Rehatsek, trans., *The Gulistan, or Rose Garden of Saʿdi* (New York, 1965), p. 134.

PUBLISHED: Anthony Welch, *Collection*, vol. 3, T. M. 3.

## 9 / A Manuscript of the *Tuhfet ul-Letaʾif*
Turkey; 1593–1594
H. 34.5 cm., W. 21.9 cm.

The twenty-one-year reign of Sultan Murad III (1574–1595) was a period of high achievement in Ottoman culture, particularly in the art of manuscript painting, of which the king was an enthusiastic and cultivated patron.[1] Manuscripts made in the imperial studio in the Topkapi Palace in Istanbul ranged widely in subject: official histories of sultans and their accomplishments; portraits of the sultans; accounts of royal festivals; books on astrology and prophecy; religious history; and works of literature. Lütfi ʿAbdullah was the director of the palace studio, and among his chief painters were Osman and ʿAli.[2]

The *Tuhfet ul-Letaʾif* is a collection of tales composed by ʿAli ibn Nakib Hamza during the reign of Sultan Murad II (1421–1451).[3] They center on the romance of Shah Ramin, son of the king of Ghazni, and Mah Parvin, daughter of the king's *vazir* Shahruz. The names of all the chief characters in the stories are Iranian, and it is likely that the author gathered together a number of episodes that were popular in fifteenth-century Turkey and Iran. Nothing is known of the author save his name, and this manuscript is apparently the only extant copy of his work, which in itself gives it great literary and bibliographic significance. It is also one of the finest illustrated manuscripts from the sixteenth-century Ottoman Empire, and therefore a work of major importance for the history of Ottoman and Islamic art. The text is written in a simple, popular prose with occasional passages of poetry. Although the colophon does not name the scribe, who copied the book in a very firm, clear, large *naskh*, it states in a versified chronogram that the manuscript was produced in the palace studio of Murad III and finished in the year 1593–1594 (A.H. 1002). The book comprises three hundred pages and is illustrated with eight double-page and sixty-one single-page paintings. None of the pictures is signed, but their high quality makes it likely that artists of the stature of Lütfi ʿAbdullah and Osman were among the illustrators. The volume was bound by a master binder. The following pages are illustrated here:

**9** / folio 177b: Mah Parvin and Ruzbin receive pearls from human-headed sea monsters (also in color)

**9** / folios 226b–227a: Saruye Shah summons the demons to aid him against Shah Ramin

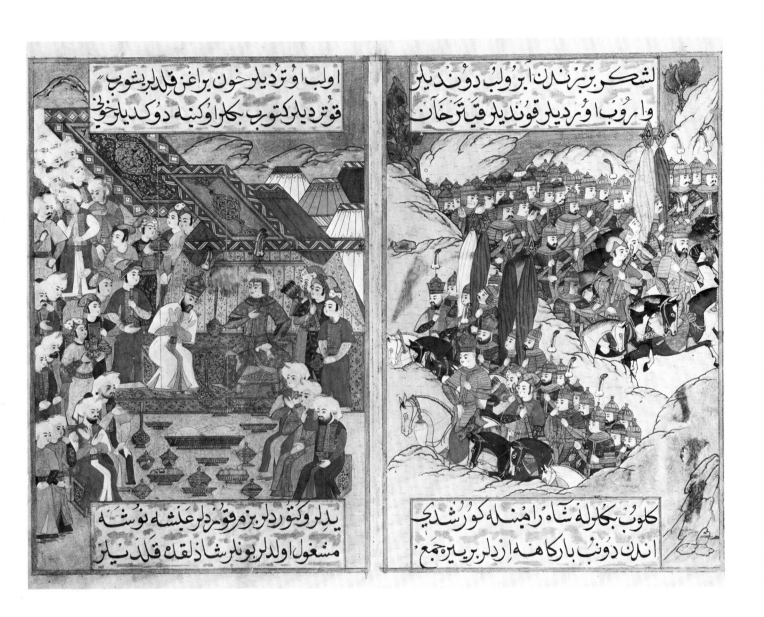

9 / folios 252b–253a: Kayter Khan receives Shah Ramin in his pavilion

fol. 177b:          Mah Parvin and Ruzbin receive pearls from human-headed sea monsters.

fols. 226b–227a:    Saruye Shah summons the demons to aid him against Shah Ramin.

fols. 252b–253a:    Kayter Khan receives Shah Ramin in his pavilion.

A. W.

1. See Nurhan Atasoy and Filiz Çagman, *Turkish Miniature Painting* (Istanbul, 1974), pp. 31–54 and pls. 12–29.

2. Cat. no. 7 has been attributed to 'Ali.

3. There is no information about the *Tuhfet ul-Leta'if* other than what is provided by the author in the manuscript itself. This entry is based almost entirely upon the preliminary research of G. M. Meredith-Owens, to whom the authors are profoundly grateful.

## 10 / Musical Gathering

Turkey, Istanbul; early 18th century
Page: H. 38.2 cm., W. 24.4 cm.
Miniature: H. 26.4 cm., W. 17 cm.

Instrumental music is frequently depicted in Islamic painting, with the musicians shown either as figures in larger gatherings[1] or alone.[2] Here we see two players—a young man with tambourine and a young woman with an *ektar*—but since two of the three standing women look toward the left, this picture may have been the right half of a double-page frontispiece whose left side would have revealed the audience, either a small court party or two princely lovers.[3] The two cypresses and the flowering trees (their blossoms looking like sugar wafers) are standard love-metaphors in Islamic painting, and the dense, allover blanket of grass and plants is typical of later Ottoman work.

Earlier Ottoman painting focused on naturalistic accounts of military campaigns,[4] natural settings, court ceremonials, and officials and sultans.[5] This factual and mundane emphasis was altered during the reign of Sultan Ahmad III (1703–1730), who maintained a sophisticated atelier dominated by his refined taste, which tended toward themes more akin to those in seventeenth-century Iranian painting. During the so-called Tulip Period (1718–1730), themes of worldly elegance, courtly amusements, and idle beauty predominate, in striking contrast with the largely heroic and official content of earlier Ottoman painting.

A. W.

1. See cat. no. 37.

2. See cat. no. 27.

3. In the Musée du Louvre is a nearly identical picture with less fine brushwork and a small kneeling figure in the lower left. It is a modified copy of the painting illustrated here.

4. See cat. no. 7.

5. See cat. no. 6.

PUBLISHED: Anthony Welch, *Collection*, vol. 3, T. M. 4.

# *Iran*

By the end of the ninth century—some two hundred and fifty years after the Muslim conquest—Iran had become one of the major creative centers of Islamic culture. Ceramics provide us with almost all our knowledge about Iranian painting before the end of the thirteenth century, but abundant extant calligraphies establish the Seljuq period (ca. 1055–1258) as one of the great creative eras for the arts of the pen as well. The Mongol invasions of the thirteenth century devastated Iran; not for decades did the land recover. Reigning under the dynastic name of Il-Khans, the descendants of the Mongols became some of Iran's great patrons of the arts of the book, and the sixteenth-century painter Dust Muhammad looked back at the Il-Khanid age as the formative period of Iranian figural painting. Under Timurid kings and princes of the fifteenth century an ideal of royal patronage was established that remained fundamentally important for later painting in Iran and India. Of the many urban centers throughout Iran where painting flourished, the most important were Tabriz and Herat, at the end of the century the home of Bihzad, the most renowned of Islamic painters.

Under the rule of the Safavi dynasty after 1501, Iran became a Shi'a Muslim state. The Prophet's son-in-law 'Ali was now regarded as the first painter, as well as first calligrapher, and under several Safavid patrons the status of painting and painters approached that of calligraphy and calligraphers. Shah Tahmasp (r. 1524–1576) is unquestionably the Safavis' great patron of painting, and for the first twenty years of his reign he carefully assembled a brilliant atelier and directed its various traditions toward a creative synthesis of styles. The process can be read in his greatest achievement, the Houghton *Shahnamah*—the most sumptuous manuscript of the *Shahnamah* ever produced and one of the greatest treasures of world art. When in mid-reign the shah lost interest in these arts, a number of court artists emigrated to the Ottoman and Mughal empires, where they were instrumental in the creation of new styles for new patrons. Others sought alternative patronage within Iran, particularly at the court of Tahmasp's brilliant nephew Ibrahim.

During the brief reign of Tahmasp's successor Isma'il II (1576–1577) the tradition of the royal *Shahnamah* continued, but later Safavid painting under Shah ʿAbbas I (r. 1587–1629) and his successors was marked by increasing diversity of patronage, with the king's personal aesthetic no longer exercising as dominant a role. Shahs, princes, aristocrats, merchants, soldiers, officials, professionals, and artists numbered among late sixteenth- and seventeenth-century patrons, and they largely turned their support from lengthy illustrated manuscripts to less time-consuming and less expensive single-page paintings and drawings, intended to be bound in albums. This development of individual, self-contained pictures as works of art was also underway in contemporary India. In both states these transformations in patronage and format were accompanied by a heightened sense of artistic self-awareness, expressed through more signed or ascribed work and through an increase in the number of art-historical chronicles. Europe, and to a lesser extent India, affected Iranian painting style in the seventeenth century, but Europeanizing became most pronounced under the nineteenth-century Qajar dynasty. It was then, too, that the widespread adoption of printing eroded the traditional art and patronage of calligraphy, painting, and the precious book.

A. W.

## 11 / Page from a Qur'an

Iran; late 11th century
Page: H. 30.7 cm., W. 22.7 cm.
Calligraphy: H. 21.7 cm., W. 14.5 cm.

What is loosely called Kufic—the heavy, angular, and monumental style of Arabic script that was used in all Qur'ans until the eleventh century—had many variants, all written according to careful canons of proportion and rhythm. The unfortunately dispersed manuscript from which this page comes was one of the great achievements of Qur'anic calligraphy and Iranian culture. Light blue tendrils form a dense but delicately drawn background that opens up into lush blossoms. Across this image of natural beauty, its balanced composition perhaps intended to reflect divine order, moves the measured elegance of the text. The verses illustrated here, from the Qur'an's *surah al-Ma'idah* (5:44–45), deal with Allah's earlier revelation of the Torah. The text on the two sides of this page begins on the reverse and continues on the side illustrated:

> (*reverse*)  . . . as they were bidden to observe,
> and thereunto were they witnesses.
> So fear not mankind, but fear Me.
> And barter not My revelations for a
> little gain. Whoso judgeth not by
> that which Allah hath revealed:

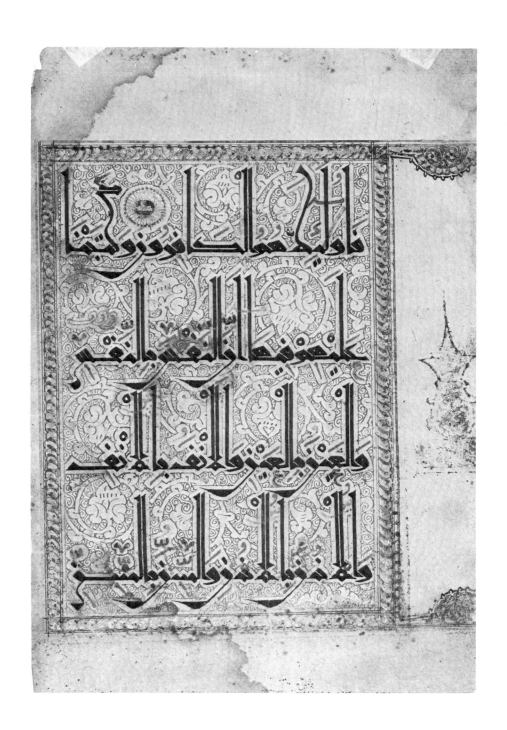

(*obverse*)   such are disbelievers.
   And We prescribed for them therein:
The life for the life, and the eye for
the eye, and the nose for the nose,
and the ear for the ear, and the
tooth for the tooth, and for wounds. . . .[1]

 The text is written on paper, and the script style resembles the Kufic on Samanid pottery bowls of the same period.[2] It is probably correct to assume that this manuscript was also produced in northeastern Iran, perhaps in Mashhad, where at least one other Qur'an in a closely allied style was written.[3] The Kufic here is composed of steep, strong, and mostly straight verticals, with compacted horizontals that hug their base line. Those letters that descend below the line do so almost invariably with an incisive cut. The whole effect is one of discipline, control, and stately self-assurance. It is an aesthetic entirely suited to the scripture that formed the basis of Islamic societies.

A. W.

1. Marmaduke Pickthall, trans., *The Glorious Koran* (London, 1976), p. 144.
2. For a recent discussion of these bowls, see Anthony Welch, *Calligraphy in the Arts of the Muslim World* (Austin and London, 1979), nos. 9, 10.
3. For another page from this Qur'an and a discussion of the related Mashhad Qur'an, see Welch, *Calligraphy*, no. 13, where other pages dispersed among many private and public collections are listed.

## 12 / Fragment of a Qur'an
Iraq or Iran; 12th century
Page: H. 25.4 cm., W. 19.5 cm.

 This double page begins the thirtieth and final *juz'* (section) of the Qur'an. It commences with the initial verses from the *surah al-Naba'* (Tidings), 78:1–5, which warns disbelievers of the pains awaiting them in the hereafter:

In the name of Allah, the Beneficent, the
 Merciful.
Whereof do they question one another?
(It is) of the awful tidings,
Concerning which they are in disagreement.
Nay, but they will come to know!
Nay, again, but they will come to know!

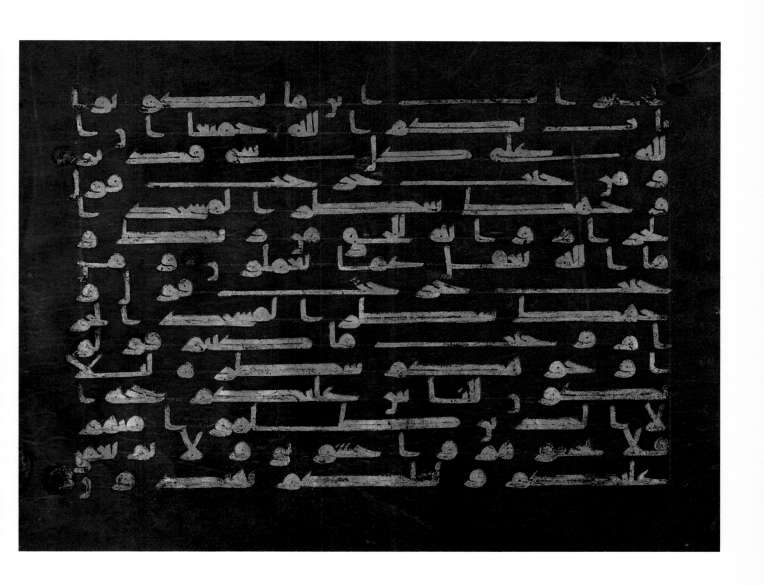

Page from a Qur'an. Cat. no. 1

Portrait of Sultan Selim II. Cat. no. 6

Mah Parvin and Ruzbin receive pearls from human-headed sea monsters. Cat.
no. 9, folio 177b

Fragment of a Qur'an. Cat. no. 12

*Lovers in a Storm.* Cat. no. 21

Firdausi encounters the court poets of Ghazna. Cat. no. 22(A)

Rustam pursues Akvan the onager-*div*. Cat. no. 22(B)

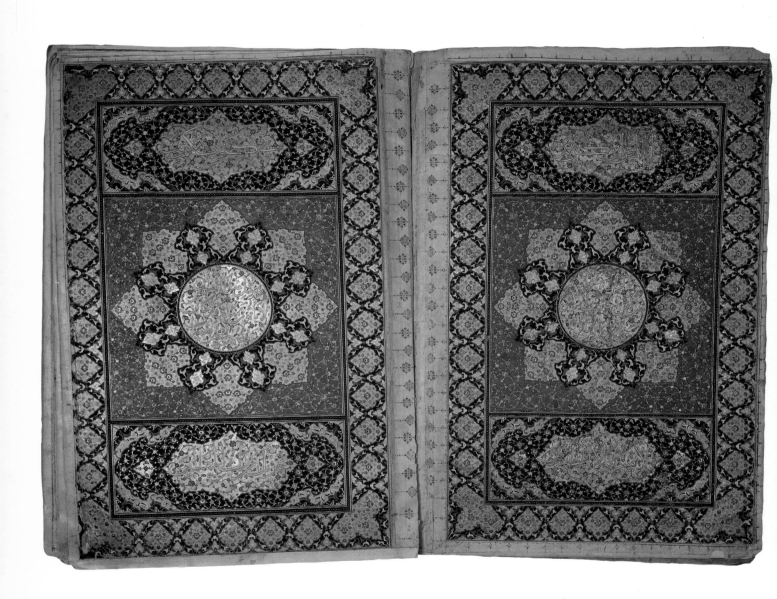

A manuscript of the Qur'an. Cat. no. 26

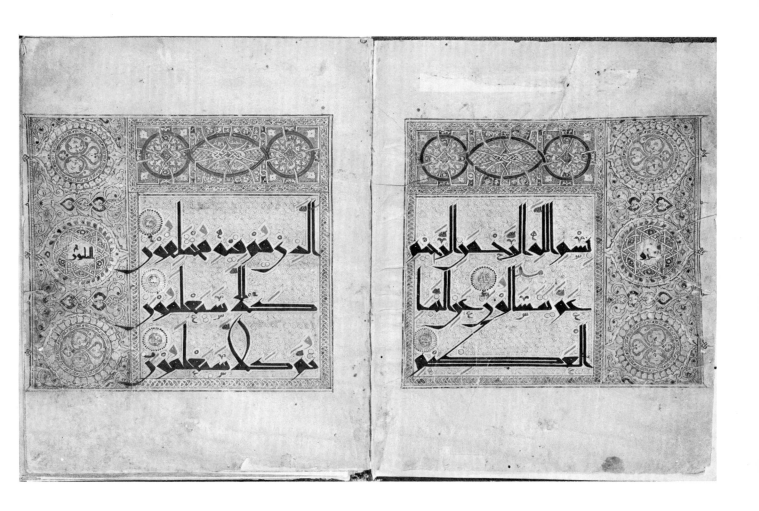

**12** / (also in color)

Thirty-four additional pages, most of them nonsequential, are bound in a simple leather binding of the late eighteenth or nineteenth century. They include two other illuminated pages and ten illuminated *surah* (chapter) headings. No other pages from this great medieval Qur'an are known; but the surviving thirty-six pages give ample indication that it was one of the finest achievements of Qur'anic calligraphy and illumination.

To the unknown scribe, aesthetic criteria were more significant than easy legibility; for those letters particularly difficult to read he supplied, directly above or below, a small light blue equivalent in *naskh* style, legibly written in its independent form. Vowels and diacritical marks are added in bright red, providing a lively counterpoint of color to the somber black Kufic. The cursive, curvilinear *naskh* had long emerged from clerical use into acceptability as a formal script style, but the monumental Kufic was still preferred for stone epigraphs or for lapidary elegance on light brown paper Qur'ans. Here, against a muted and discreet repetitive background of tiny arabesques, the script moves with sonorous stateliness, confining itself within its right-hand, upper, and lower borders but asserting preeminence by overrunning the illuminated margins on the left. Elongated horizontals, emphatic diagonals, and deliberately aligned verticals create a compelling sequence of stark beauty.

Although the script is uniformly impressive throughout the surviving pages of this great Qur'an, the opening of the thirtieth *juz'* (and, presumably, of the twenty-nine sections that have not survived) required illumination, and the illuminator was an artist of the highest caliber. The two halves are mirror-images, rendered with impressive exactitude. In the far right- and left-hand margins are three *ansas* (roundels): the two central medallions identify the *juz'*, and the other four are filled with carefully balanced vegetal arabesques. The upper border, directly over the written portion of each page, is bounded by intertwined gold "chains" and contains two blue circles flanking a central blue oval. Within the oval, in the interstices of extremely complex interlace, is written the basic identification of the *surah*. In these margin illuminations, intricate gold interlacing and a restrained use of blue, white, and red create complex patterns of total harmony that suggest the medieval fascination with mathematics as a distant revelation of divine order.

A. W.

Published: Anthony Welch, *Collection*, vol. 2, Ms. 2; Martin Lings and Yasin H. Safadi, *The Qur'an* (London, 1976), no. 37; Martin Lings, *The Qur'anic Art of Calligraphy and Illumination* (London, 1977), p. 18 and pl. 12; Anthony Welch, *Calligraphy in the Arts of the Muslim World* (Austin and London, 1979), no. 12.

## 13 / Bahram Gur at the House of Mahiyar the Jeweler

Iran or Iraq; ca. 1300
From a manuscript of Firdausi's *Shahnamah*
Page: H. 23.8 cm., W. 19.4 cm.
Miniature: H. 4.9 cm., W. 12 cm.

The Iranian poet Firdausi completed his sixty-thousand-verse epic, the *Shahnamah* (*Book of Kings*), about the year 1010, recounting in it the tales and exploits of Iran's pre-Islamic heroes and kings from earliest times to the seventh-century Arab Conquest. Despite the poem's wide popularity, it was apparently known primarily in oral form, for there are no extant manuscripts of it before the fourteenth century.

The first Muslim Il-Khan (Mongol ruler whose territory centered about Iran) was Ghazan Khan, who on ascending the throne in 1295 began to favor Iranians and Iranian culture. It was likely due to this impetus that unknown patrons, probably in Baghdad, commissioned illustrated copies of Firdausi's epic: pages from four of these *Shahnamahs* are preserved. Because they are small in comparison with later Il-Khanid copies of the poem, they are known as the *Small Shahnamahs*.[1] They are key documents for the formation of Iranian painting and the emergence of the precious literary manuscript as a major vehicle for princely patronage.

The text is written in a competent *naskh* in six vertical columns and deals with the visit of Shah Bahram Gur (one of the great heroes and lovers in the *Shahnamah*) to the house of Mahiyar, a wealthy jeweler. Disguised as the knight Gushasp, he sits at the left in the illustration, listening to the panegyric music of Mahiyar's daughter, Arzu, who compares him more than favorably with Shah Bahram Gur. The story ends with their marriage. The interior is richly decorated in gold, and the unknown painter has used wall hangings and placement of figures to create a sense of depth. Figural style seen here is closely related to that on contemporary metalwork and pottery.

A. W.

1. The definitive study of the *Small Shahnamahs* is M. Shreve Simpson, *The Illustration of an Epic: The Earliest Shahnama Manuscripts* (New York and London, 1979). Five other Il-Khanid *Shahnamahs* are known: the dispersed Demotte *Shahnamah* and four *Shahnamahs* produced under Inju patronage in Shiraz. There is no extant colophon for any of the four *Small Shahnamahs*. This page belonged originally to the *Second Small Shahnamah*.

PUBLISHED: Arthur Upham Pope, *Masterpieces of Persian Art* (New York, 1945), pl. 121; Anthony Welch, *Collection*, vol. 1, Ir. M. 1.

## 14 / Forest Conflict

Iran; ca. 1400–1405
Page: H. 21.1 cm., W. 32.7 cm.
Miniature: H. 8.4 cm., W. 18.5 cm.

After 1335 Il-Khan domination of Iran and adjacent areas rapidly disintegrated. The several smaller powers that succeeded it were not strong enough to repel the 1381–1392 invasions and conquest of Iran by Timur (Tamerlane). Subsequent resistance to Timurid rule in western Iran and Iraq was largely led by a gifted strategist and patron of Il-Khan descent, Sultan Ahmed Jala'ir, who struggled with Timur for control of Baghdad and Tabriz and the lands between the two cities. Like his opponent, Timur was a connoisseur of the arts and established a tradition of princely Timurid patronage that was to pass ultimately to the Mughals of India.

This tumultuous pen-and-ink drawing includes no written information about patron, artist, place of origin, or date. In the illuminated margins six panels contain inscriptions in well-composed *ta'liq* script—verses from a fine poem in *mathnawi* meter that has, however, nothing whatever to do with the drawing's subject matter and could not have been composed before the end of the fifteenth century. The drawing was produced either as a single page for an admiring connoisseur or as a leaf for a *muraqqa'* (album) of paintings, drawings, and calligraphies; the borders were pasted on at a later date.

Idyllic calm is the prevailing atmosphere in fifteenth-century illustrations of literary manuscripts. But this drawing offers only a few instances of relief from a scene of compounded desperation: the two ducks in the lower center appear quite unperturbed by the turmoil around them, while the *simurgh* above them gazes fixedly off into the distance. At the left a lion savages a deer, whose mate screams helplessly. Two monkeys chatter and gesticulate. At the right a lone, bearded man, armed only with a short knife, clutches a dragon's throat, and a pair of ducks swoops through a stormy sky. The thick vegetation is equally threatening and equally charged with energy.

This masterful drawing, perhaps illustrating an oral tale never recorded and now lost, stands near the beginning of the great Iranian tradition of draftsmanship and can be compared with other contemporary drawings.[1] It was most likely executed in northwestern Iran in the early fifteenth century. Sultan Giyath al-Din Ahmed Jala'ir, who died in 1409, may have been the patron, but there were probably other cultured Jala'irids who could have commissioned such a work.[2]

A. W.

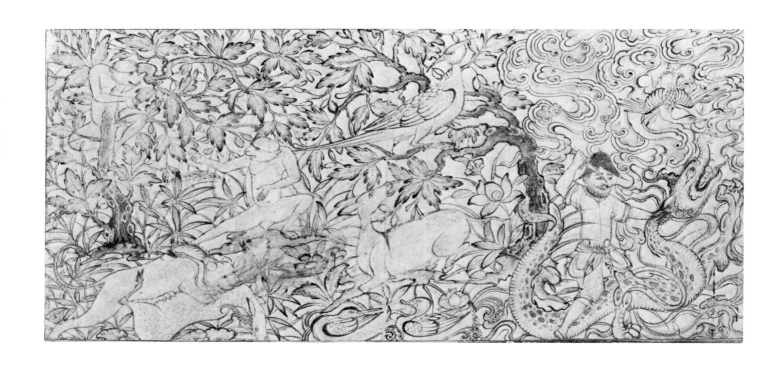

1. Two groups of albums in Istanbul and Berlin contain drawings in similar style. See M. S. Ipsiroğlu, *Saray-Alben: Diez'sche Klebebände aus den Berliner Sammlungen* (Wiesbaden, 1964); and idem, *Painting and Culture of the Mongols* (New York, 1966).

2. See cat. no. 15 and the well-known margins of the seven-page *Diwan* in the Freer Gallery of Art made for Sultan Ahmed Jala'ir (see Frederick R. Martin, *Miniatures from the Period of Timur in a Ms. of the Poems of Sultan Ahmad Jalair* [Vienna, 1926]; and Basil Gray, *Persian Painting* [Geneva, 1961], p. 149).

PUBLISHED: Phyllis Ackerman, *Guide to the Exhibition of Persian Art* (New York: The Iranian Institute, 1940), p. 203; Anthony Welch, *Collection*, vol. 1, Ir. M. 7.

## 15 / Monkeys Taunting a Lion

Iran; early 15th century
Page: H. 28.1 cm., W. 20.3 cm.
Miniature: H. 24.1 cm., W. 15.6 cm.

Two bemused monkeys reach out of a tree and tease an outraged lion by shaking leaves in his face. Although the animals dominate the composition, their humorous antics gain from the enchanted landscape with its vibrant patterns of tall grass, two furry trees, and rocks containing gentle grotesques. As in the last, less restrained, drawing, which may have been commissioned by the same Jala'irid patron, the theme may derive from such moralizing animal fables as those of the *Kalila wa Dimna*, which were popular throughout the Islamic world and were among the earliest illustrated Muslim books.

The popularity of this drawing is attested by a later copy, preserved in one of the great albums in the Topkapi Palace Museum Library in Istanbul.[1] Two other drawings from this source, one of a leopard, the other of a tiger, can be ascribed to the same spirited hand.[2] Stylistically, they belong to the school centered in Tabriz, in northwestern Iran, the western wing of Iranian painting which was to blend with that of the east, centered at Herat, in the new artistic systhesis under the Safavid dynasty.

S. C. W. and A. W.

1. Album H. 2152, 15/10.
2. See M. S. Ipsiroğlu and S. Eyuböglu, *Fatih Albumuna Bir Bakis* (Istanbul, 1955), figs. 102, 103.

PUBLISHED: Frederick R. Martin, *The Miniature Paintings and Painters of Persia, India and Turkey*, vol. 2 (London, 1912), pl. 64; Anthony Welch, *Collection*, vol. 1, Ir. M. 8.

**16** / A Manuscript of Firdausi's *Shahnamah*
Iran, Shiraz; 1457
H. 33.5 cm., W. 24.5 cm.

This well-known copy of Firdausi's epic is also well traveled. According to its colophon, the text was completed on the first day of the month of Rabi' al-Awwal 861 (27 January 1457) by the scribe Mahmud ibn Muhammad ibn Mahmud al-Jamali, and the manuscript's fifty-three illustrations clearly establish that scribe and painters were working in the southern Iranian cultural center of Shiraz, probably under the patronage of the Turcoman governor Pir Budaq.[1] Although Shiraz enjoyed a somewhat less turbulent history than Iran's capital cities, it still suffered periods of unrest during which this *Shahnamah* might have been appropriated or its owner might have spirited it away. It turned up in India, and we next hear of it in about 1775, being given to John Shore, Baron Teignmouth (1751–1834), by his instructor in Indian languages. It may have been used to teach the baron Persian. Sailing on the Ganges, Teignmouth's boat capsized, and the book was dunked: most of its margins are water-stained as a result. The rescued manuscript returned to Britain with its owner, who in old age lent it to the nineteenth-century Orientalist Sir William Ouseley. In 1952 the Teignmouth *Shahnamah* moved to New York as part of the Kevorkian collection, and in 1969 it entered Prince Sadruddin's collection.

The manuscript's 554 pages are mostly written in four columns of twenty-five lines to the page in a crisp, distinguished *nasta'liq*. All that is known about Mahmud ibn Muhammad, the scribe, is that he copied two other manuscripts, dated to 1453 and 1463.[2]

The anonymous illuminator was perhaps the most talented of the artists who worked on this *Shahnamah*. His illuminated double page beginning the text (illustrated) is a masterfully balanced creation in the Timurid tradition. The two dominant tones—dark blue and gold—are equal in emphasis, and the horizontal and vertical design patterns are intricately interlocked. In the outer margins a restrained orange and green alternate in tempered company, and the multicolored arabesque is small and strong. The two pages are nearly mirror images, but there are subtle and intriguing differences between them.

A single painter, appropriately dubbed the Teignmouth Painter by Basil W. Robinson, was responsible for fifty of the manuscript's illustrations. Despite some damage to the page, his miniature of the *simurgh* rescuing the abandoned infant Zal (fol. 33a, illustrated) indicates that he was an innovative master working within the continuing Timurid traditions of mid-fifteenth-century Shiraz. His dominant role in this manuscript, as well as his contributions to several other Shiraz manuscripts,[3] demonstrates that he was one of the city's major painters. Two other masters, working in

**16** / folios 1b–2a: Illuminated double page of text

**16** / folio 33a: The *simurgh* rescuing the abandoned infant Zal

what Robinson has termed the "Turkman" style, made less extensive additions to the book (the double-page frontispiece and two other miniatures). The Teignmouth *Shahnamah* is not only one of the earliest books produced for a Turcoman patron in Shiraz, it is also the major opus of the Teignmouth Painter and one of the few manuscripts that contain pictures in both the traditional Shiraz and the new "Turkman" styles.

A. W.

1. The scholarly significance of this manuscript has been established by Basil W. Robinson in several publications: *Persian Paintings* (London, 1951); *Persian Drawings* (New York, 1965), pp. 26–28; and *Persian Miniature Painting* (London, 1967), pp. 90–95.

2. In 1453 (A.H. 857) Mahmud ibn Muhammad copied a *Diwan* of Qasim al-Anwar, now in the Nationalbibliothek, Vienna, and in 1463 (A.H. 867) a *Khamsah* of Amir Khusraw Dehlevi, now in the Bodleian Library, Oxford.

3. Robinson has attributed the illustrations of three other manuscripts to him: a *Kulliyat* of Sa'di produced in 1448 (A.H. 852), in the Chester Beatty Library, Dublin; an undated *Khamsah* of Nizami, in the Bibliothèque Nationale, Paris; and an undated *Khamsah* of Nizami, in the Topkapi Palace Museum, Istanbul.

PUBLISHED: Robinson, *Persian Paintings;* Welch, *Collection,* vol. 4, Ms. 11.

## 17 / Golandam and a Man Who Loves Her

Iran; 1477
From a manuscript of Ibn Husam's *Khawarannamah*
Page: H. 40 cm., W. 29.2 cm.
Miniature: H. 20.5 cm., W. 28.4 cm.

Sitting in a stream flowing past a cypress and a flowering tree is a half-clothed man, his outer garments and his turban neatly laid on the ground behind him. The foliage is dense and diverse in kind—broad-leafed plants of various sorts with scattered orange blossoms, all of them flat and rather two-dimensional. From the tent at the left comes a woman in blue who is partially concealing her face. Tents and figures are likewise rendered with little sense of depth or volume. The text is written in a good *nasta'liq*.

The illustration originally belonged to a copy of the *Khawarannamah* of Ibn Husam, an epic life of 'Ali, the Prophet Muhammad's cousin and son-in-law and one of the central saints and heroes of Shi'a Islam. It is composed in the same meter as Firdausi's *Shahnamah*. It is probable that the manuscript was copied and illustrated in a Sufi center near Herat in present-day Afghanistan.[1] Its illustrations reflect one of several styles of painting current in late fifteenth-century Iran that had a formative influence on the development of Safavid painting.[2]

A. W.

1. See Yahya Zoka, "Khawaran Nama," *Hunar u Mardom*, no. 20, pp. 17–29.

2. See Stuart C. Welch, *A King's Book of Kings* (New York, 1972), p. 44; and the fuller discussion in Martin B. Dickson and Stuart C. Welch, *The Houghton Shahnameh* (Cambridge, Mass., 1981), 1:24–26, 32, 34, 41, 72, 74, 213, 238 n. 7, 239 n. 2, 244 n. 22.

PUBLISHED: Anthony Welch, *Collection*, vol. 1, Ir. M. 13.

## 18 / Two pages from a *Shahnamah* for Sultan Mirza ʿAli
Iran, Gilan; 1499
(A) Zawarah in the Hunting Ground of Siyavush
(B) Rustam Fells Ashkabus
Page: H. 34.6 cm., W. 24.5 cm.
Miniature: H. 23.4 cm., W. 15.2 cm.

There was an impressive diversity of art and patronage in late fifteenth-century Iran. The Timurids in their capital of Herat in the east supported the logical and brilliantly naturalistic painting of Bihzad, while the Aq Qoyunlu Turcomans in Tabriz in the west encouraged less cerebral and more evocative art. Provincial areas, without long traditions of independent politics or art, were active too; among them was Gilan, on the southern shores of the Caspian. In 1499 a *Shahnamah* of enormous size, originally containing about 350 illustrations in 2 volumes, was completed for Sultan Mirza ʿAli, who included on the colophon his name and that of the scribe, Salik ibn Saʿid, a competent though not outstanding master.[1] Many painters provided the illustrations: the sultan obviously supported a large and vigorous atelier.

From this atelier, by two unidentified artists, come the two paintings illustrated here. Master A was clearly more interested in a complex landscape than in spatial logic: the horse at the left has no legs; the central soldier hovers above the ground; while the horse at the right has become hopelessly entangled as it floats through the branches.

Master B seeks to avoid spatial problems altogether. He presents an essentially empty plain, made remarkable by a pattern of coursing arrows from Rustam's Iranians on the right and Ashkabus's Turanians at the left. But as our eyes move up and off the "ladder" of arrows, our attention is held by intricate rocks in the background: these are filled with animal and human faces endowed with far more individuality and vitality than those of the fighting warriors. The product of a century-old Iranian tradition, these face-enlivened rocks continue as an important element in Iranian painting well into the sixteenth century.

A. W.

**18A** / Zawarah in the hunting ground of Siyavush

**18B** / Rustam fells Ashkabus

1. The two volumes of the manuscript are now divided between the Museum of Turkish and Islamic Art (Ms. no. 1973) and the University Library (Ms. no. 7954), both in Istanbul. A large number of illustrations were removed from the *Shahnamah* about sixty years ago. For a discussion of this manuscript, see Martin B. Dickson and Stuart C. Welch, *The Houghton Shahnameh* (Cambridge, Mass., 1981), 1:27, 239 n. 2.

PUBLISHED: Anthony Welch, *Collection*, vol. 3, Ir. M. 60 and Ir. M. 60/A.

## 19 / Two Lynx and Two Antelope
By Bihzad
Iran, Herat; ca. 1495
Page: H. 9.5 cm., W. 13.3 cm.
Miniature: H. 6.7 cm., W. 12 cm.

Apparently salvaged from a larger drawing, this small work was subsequently mounted in an album, almost certainly the royal *muraqqa'* compiled on the order of Shah Tahmasp's brother Bahram Mirza by the painter and calligrapher Dust Muhammad in 1546.[1] It was probably then that this fragment was supplied with the information at the top: "A picture by the humble Bihzad after the work of Maulana Wali."[2] Bihzad is traditionally regarded as the greatest of Iranian painters. He dominated Timurid and Safavid court ateliers in Herat and Tabriz for more than forty years and is the subject of generally approving comment in many sixteenth-century sources. Although his contemporary, Maulana Wali, is seldom mentioned, Bihzad himself obviously regarded him as a talent worth copying. The most significant reference to him is by the Mughal emperor Babur's cousin, Mirza Muhammad Haydar Dughlat: "Master Shaykh Ahmad, brother of Baba Haji, and Maulana Junayd and Master Husam al-Din the poignard maker, and Maulana Wali—all these are skilled masters and no one of them is superior to the other."[3]

The pose of the two deer suggests that Bihzad addressed his admiration to Maulana Wali's illustration of "Bahram Gur's Master Shot," one of the more spectacular hunting episodes in Firdausi's *Shahnamah.* Neither rock nor tree conforms to usual notions of Bihzad's art but instead reflects more conventional Timurid types: Maulana Wali must have been a more traditional artist.

On the reverse are four lines of poetry, followed by an illuminated heading and a portion of a colophon. The colophon does not identify the text but does mention the scribe, Sultan Muhammad Khandan, one of the eminent early Safavid calligraphers, and gives a date equivalent to March–April 1502.

A. W. and S. C. W.

19

1. The Bahram Mirza album is discussed in Stuart C. Welch, *A King's Book of Kings* (New York, 1972), p. 16; a far more thorough discussion appears in Martin B. Dickson and Stuart C. Welch, *The Houghton Shahnameh* (Cambridge, Mass., 1981; see index to vol. 1).

2. For additional information on Bihzad, see cat. no. 20, which appears also to have belonged to the Bahram Mirza album and to have been likewise inscribed by Dust Muhammad.

3. The *Ta'rikh-i Rashidi,* trans. T. W. Arnold, in Laurence Binyon, J. V. S. Wilkinson, and Basil Gray, *Persian Miniature Painting* (London, 1933), pp. 189–91.

PUBLISHED: Armenag Sakisian, *La Miniature persane* (Paris and Brussels, 1929), pl. 75, fig. 134; Anthony Welch, *Collection,* vol. 3, Ir. M. 64.

## 20 / Portrait of Hatifi

By Bihzad
Iran; 1511–1521
Page: H. 11.8 cm., W. 7.7 cm.
Miniature: H. 9.4 cm., W. 6 cm.

"A portrait of Maulana 'Abdullah Hatifi. The work of Master Bihzad." This inscription above and below the painting was written about 1546 by the Safavid painter-calligrapher Dust Muhammad, who chose to include this tiny portrait in the great album he put together for Bahram Mirza, the brother of Shah Tahmasp.[1] It supplies crucial information, and there seems no reason to doubt its authenticity.

Hatifi was the son of the sister of Jami, the mystical poet who enjoyed the patronage of Sultan Husayn Bayqara in late fifteenth-century Herat. Though less famed than his uncle, Hatifi enjoyed a considerable reputation. He was the author of a *Timurnamah* (an epic celebrating the exploits of Tamerlane), which he tactfully composed for his Timurid patron, Sultan Husayn, and also of several other long poems on traditional themes. A Shi'a Muslim, Hatifi was visited in 1511 by the first Safavid shah, Isma'il, who had conquered Herat and the province of Khurasan. On that occasion the poet recited a thousand-line panegyric on his new king, and it is likely that the present portrait commemorates the event. The turban he wears in this portrait includes the characteristic baton of the Safavids, presumably donned by the poet to proclaim his allegiance.

Bihzad was probably born about the middle of the fifteenth century in or near Herat, and his talent was recognized early. His initial patron appears to have been Mir 'Ali Shir Nawa'i, the great poet and *vazir* of Sultan Husayn Bayqara, but by 1485 he was receiving commissions from the sultan himself. He continued in Timurid service until 1507, when Herat was conquered by the Uzbeks, for whose leader, Shaybani Khan, he presumably worked until the city fell to the Safavids in 1510. The future Shah Tahmasp was appointed nominal governor of the city in 1516, when he was not quite two years old; he returned to the Safavid capital at Tabriz in 1522 accom-

panied by Bihzad, who was subsequently appointed director of the royal library. He clearly had a hand in training Tahmasp as a painter, and he exercised enormous influence over the development of Safavid painting. He died in 1536.

Bihzad was a masterful observer of hands, and Hatifi's gesture in this portrait conveys a gentle self-assurance and composure appropriate to a man who had known years of high favor. His face is lined; his eyes are tired; and his beard is rendered in a meticulous blend of tones, characteristic of Bihzad's precision.

S. C. W. and A. W.

1. On the reverse is a fragment of superb illumination, datable to about 1540. This miniature is discussed at length in Martin B. Dickson and Stuart C. Welch, *The Houghton Shahnameh* (Cambridge, Mass., 1981), 1:34, 193, 240 n. 12.

PUBLISHED: Armenag Sakisian, *La Miniature persane* (Paris and Brussels, 1929), pl. 74 and fig. 129.

## 21 / Lovers in a Storm

Attrib. to Shaykh Zadah
Iran, Tabriz; ca. 1525
From a manuscript of the *Diwan* of Sana'i
Page: H. 29.3 cm., W. 19.5 cm.
Miniature: H. 18 cm., W. 11.2 cm.

On the reverse of this miniature is a poem describing a journey, from the *Diwan* of Sana'i, a Persian mystical poet who died in 1131. This painting was presumably once part of an illustrated manuscript of Sana'i's *Diwan* made for the young Safavid ruler, Shah Tahmasp (r. 1524–1576), who commissioned sumptuous editions of many classics of Iranian literature during the first two decades of his reign.[1] It can be attributed on grounds of style to Shaykh Zadah, a major court artist who was the most faithful follower of Bihzad.[2] Both came into Tahmasp's service in Tabriz in 1522, and Shaykh Zadah contributed a large number of paintings to the manuscripts produced under Tahmasp's aegis until the latter 1520s, when he left Tabriz in order to join the Uzbeks at Bukhara.

Two comically monstrous demons create a storm of wind and rain to assail a ship carrying a pair of lovers, four other passengers, and a crew of three. The landscape is sparse and ambiguous, though rendered with total clarity; spatial relationships and emotional conditions are expressively defined. The figures so closely resemble those in a painting ascribed to Shaykh Zadah in a *Diwan* of the poet Hafiz, copied about 1527, that this unsigned picture could only be by Shaykh Zadah. This copy of Sana'i's

21 / (also in color)

*Diwan* must have been produced during the years when Shaykh Zadah was at the high point of his career.

S. C. W. and A. W.

1. Paintings signed by or attributed to Shaykh Zadah occur in a number of them: the ca. 1525 *Khamsah* of Nizami (Metropolitan Museum of Art, New York), the 1526 *Diwan* of Mir ʿAli Shir Nawaʾi (Bibliothèque Nationale, Paris), and the ca. 1527 *Diwan* of Hafiz (Fogg Art Museum, Cambridge, Mass., and private collections). For a discussion of this artist, see Martin B. Dickson and Stuart C. Welch, *The Houghton Shahnameh* (Cambridge, Mass., 1981), vol. 1, particularly pp. 37–39.
2. See cat. no. 20.

PUBLISHED: Phyllis Ackerman, *Guide to the Exhibition of Persian Art* (New York: The Iranian Institute, 1940), p. 195; Ernst Grube, *Muslim Miniature Painting* (Venice, 1962), no. 58; Anthony Welch, *Catalogue*, vol. 3, Ir. M. 63.

## 22 / Two Pages from a *Shahnamah* for Shah Tahmasp

(A) Firdausi Encounters the Court Poets of Ghazna
    (folio 7a)
    Attrib. to Aqa Mirak
    Iran, Tabriz; ca. 1532
    Miniature: H. 26.7 cm., W. 23.2 cm.
(B) Rustam Pursues Akvan the Onager-*Div* (folio 294a)
    Attrib. to Muzaffar ʿAli
    Iran, Tabriz; ca. 1530–1535
    Miniature: H. 26.8 cm., W. 17.3 cm.

These miniatures were among the 258 commissioned for a splendid copy of the poet Firdausi's epic, the *Shahnamah (Book of Kings)*, at Tabriz between about 1522 and 1540. Probably initiated by Shah Ismaʿil (r. 1501–1524), founder of the Safavid state, the project was carried on and completed for his son and successor Shah Tahmasp (r. 1524–1576). Although he was for years an enthusiastic painter as well as a deeply creative patron, Shah Tahmasp eventually forsook the art to concentrate upon piety and statecraft. In 1568 he presented this manuscript to the Ottoman Sultan Selim II. By 1903 it had left the Ottoman royal library and belonged to Baron Edmond de Rothschild, one of whose descendants sold it in 1959 to Arthur A. Houghton, Jr., after whom it is now known as the Houghton *Shahnamah*.

In the first painting, Firdausi is seen encountering the court poets of Sultan Mahmud of Ghazna, whose royal patronage he sought in order to complete the great Iranian epic. At first rude and suspicious, the picnicking poets challenged their visitor to cap a particularly difficult verse, a feat he accomplished so brilliantly that they reluctantly accepted him. Later, he met the sultan, impressed him, and was granted his patronage. The *Shahnamah* was finished in A.D. 1010.

**22A** / Firdausi encounters the court poets of Ghazna (also in color)

**22B** / Rustam pursues Akvan the onager-*div* (also in color)

Crisp, bright, and boldly composed as a handful of jewels scattered across the page, this miniature provides a lyrical yet majestic fanfare for the shah's grandest manuscript, to which it is the first illustration. Although such major artists as Aqa Mirak often employed assistants to color their designs or carry out lesser passages, this painting is entirely his work, a true masterpiece down to the last tuft of grass. It contains a portrait of the shah as a beardless young man, standing behind the poets at the right side of the composition. Inasmuch as Aqa Mirak, to whom we ascribe the picture on grounds of style, was on terms of friendship as well as service with his patron and was also a noted portrait painter, it is not surprising that he was honored with this prestigious assignment. Happily, Aqa Mirak was retained in the royal ateliers during the years of Shah Tahmasp's disinclination for painting. For a large miniature for a *Falnamah* designed and partly carried out by him, see catalogue number 25.

In a second miniature from this *Shahnamah* we see the illustrious Iranian hero Rustam bearing down upon the wicked and wily Akvan, a *div* (demon) who had taken on the form of an onager, or wild ass, and was attacking the herds of the Iranian shah Kay Khusraw. Akvan turned, snakelike, and sighted his pursuer, and just as Rustam's lasso touched him, he vanished.

Muzaffar 'Ali, to whom we assign this miniature, was of the second generation in the Safavid ateliers. Admired as a spiritual luminary, calligrapher, and chess player as well as artist, he united all his talents in this miniature. Its soaring buoyancy of design not only reveals a chess player's artful planning but transcends the mere illustration of a spritely episode. Seeing it raises our spirits, and no small measure of the artist's accomplishment stems from his mastery of calligraphy's graceful curves, tripping runs, and snappy rhythms.

The artist's grasp of animal psychology, as well as movement, can be seen in the hatefully clever look of Akvan in contrast with the blithe innocence of the horses.

S. C. W.

PUBLISHED: Stuart C. Welch, *A King's Book of Kings* (New York, 1972), pp. 80–83, 160–63; idem, *Wonders of the Age* (Cambridge, Mass., 1979), frontispiece, pp. 42–43, 86–87; Martin B. Dickson and Stuart C. Welch, *The Houghton Shahnameh* (Cambridge, Mass., 1981), vol. 1, frontispiece, figs. 151, 215, vol. 2, pls. 2, 168.

## 23 / A Manuscript of the *Khamsah* of Nizami
Iran, Shiraz; 1527
H. 33.5 cm., W. 20.2 cm.

Shiraz was a major center of Iranian calligraphy and book illustration in the fourteenth and fifteenth centuries, and it continued to preserve its

**23** / folio 66a: Battle between Khusraw and Bahram Chubinah

regional identity well into the sixteenth century. This impressive man-uscript of 404 pages has a black leather binding, contemporary with the book, on whose spine are verses extolling Nizami's poetry. According to the book's colophon, the *nasta'liq* text was written by Pir Husayn ibn Pir Hasan al-Katib al-Shirazi.[1] The book's illumination is of very high quality, and it contains, as well, twenty-seven miniatures, all by the same painter who signed the manuscript's final illustration (fol. 383a) "Ghiyath Mudhahhib" (The Gilder).[2]

As the *Battle between Khusraw and Bahram Chubinah* indicates (fol. 66a, illustrated), he was an artist still relatively untouched by the new painting style evolving in the capital city, Tabriz, under the aegis of Shah Tahmasp. The manuscript's patron is not named. No Safavid prince was then resident in Shiraz, and the book was presumably produced for a highly placed aristocrat or for the city's governor.

A. W.

1. This scribe may possibly be identified with the copyist of a *Shahnamah* dated to 1497 (A.H. 902) in Shiraz (see Basil W. Robinson, *A Descriptive Catalogue of the Persian Paintings in the Bodleian Library* [Oxford, 1958], p. 61).

2. Ibid., p. 120, cites an illuminator by the name of Ghiyath al-Din Mahmud al-Shirazi in a *Gulistan and Bustan* of Sa'di dated to 1537 (A.H. 943). He may also be the master discussed by the late sixteenth-century chronicler Qadi Ahmad (*Calligraphers and Painters*, trans. Vladimir Minorsky [Washington, D.C., 1959], p. 189): "Maulana Ghiyath al-Din Muhammad Mudhahhib of Mashhad, the inventor of gold sprinkling, was unrivaled in painting and (ornamental) gilding. He was the contemporary of the late Maulana Sultan 'Ali Mashhadi. He died on the last day of Jamadi I 942 (26 November 1535) in Holy Mashhad and was buried beside Maulana Sultan 'Ali."

PUBLISHED: Anthony Welch, *Collection*, vol. 4, Ms. 15.

## 24 / A Love Poem

By Shah Mahmud Nishapuri (1487–1564/65)
Iran, Tabriz or Mashhad; ca. 1540–1550
Page: H. 26.6 cm., W. 16.7 cm.
Calligraphy: H. 17.4 cm., W. 6.7 cm.

This elegant work was originally designed either as a single page or for inclusion in a *muraqqa'* (album). It can be equally praised for its blue mar-bleized and gold-flecked margins, its delicate floral corner illuminations, and its *nasta'liq* style of script, identified in the lower left as the work of Shah Mahmud Nishapuri, one of the foremost Safavid calligraphers and, like many of his colleagues, a poet of reputed ability. One assumes that this particular mediocre poem does not number among the efforts that earned him a literary reputation:

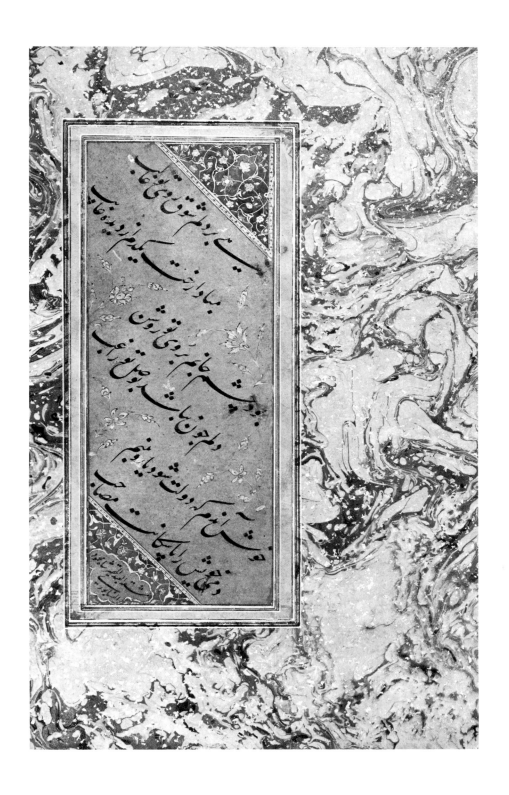

O you, longing for whose face overwhelms my heart,
May your face never be absent from my eyes.
Since my soul's eye becomes radiant from your face,
How could my heart not covet union with you?
Happy that moment, when fortune became my friend,
And I see myself for a moment as a companion of
    your days![1]

The quality of calligraphy indicates why the late-sixteenth-century chronicler of the arts, Qadi Ahmad, felt justified in including Shah Mahmud (who had earned from Shah Tahmasp the honorific title Zarin Qalam, or Golden Pen) with Sultan ʿAli and Mir ʿAli as one of the three great masters of early Safavid script.[2] Evoking the world's gentler motions, like falling leaves or ripples in a stream, nastaʿliq was in the sixteenth century the favored style of script for most of Iran's great poetical manuscripts, as well as for its lesser and smaller works of lyric poetry.

Qadi Ahmad is our chief source of knowledge for the scribe, since he studied with Shah Mahmud on and off during the last eight years of the calligrapher's life. Shah Mahmud was born in 1487 (A.H. 892) in Nishapur and studied the art of writing under his uncle Maulana ʿAbdi, who later attained high position at the court of Shah Tahmasp (r. 1524–1576). Through his talent and training and his uncle's connections Shah Mahmud also got a post at the king's court in Tabriz in the late 1520s, when the shah was devoting much of his time to the supervision of the arts. Qadi Ahmad specifically cites Shah Mahmud as the scribe of a copy of Nizami's Khamsah, illustrated by the famed painter Bihzad; a later copy of the Khamsah, dated to 1539–1543 and adorned with works by the greatest painters of the Safavid court, bears his name on the colophon. He was a pious man: while in the king's employ, he lived in a Tabriz madrasa (theological seminary), and after the shah lost interest in painting and calligraphy about 1545, the scribe moved to the great Shiʿa holy city of Mashhad, where he again inhabited a madrasa. He never married but preferred a reclusive life and in Mashhad supported himself by teaching and selling specimens of his art (of which this page may have been one) until his death in 1564–1565 (A.H. 972).

A. W.

1. We are indebted to Annemarie Schimmel for identifying and translating this poem.
2. Qadi Ahmad, Calligraphers and Painters, trans. Vladimir Minorsky (Washington, D.C., 1959), pp. 135–38.

PUBLISHED: Phyllis Ackerman, Guide to the Exhibition of Persian Art (New York: The Iranian Institute, 1940).

**25** / A King Chased from the Tomb of a Saint
By Aqa Mirak
Iran; mid-16th century
From a manuscript of the *Falnamah*
Page and miniature: H. 59.5 cm., W. 45 cm.

This dynamic giant miniature is from a copy of the *Falnamah* (Book of Divination), traditionally ascribed, along with a number of other popular works on divination, magic, and alchemy, to the Shi'a imam Ja'far al-Sadiq. The text consists of omens and predictions arranged under the names of twenty-five prophets. Though princely patrons more often selected works of history or literary classics for illustration in their ateliers, numerous royal copies of texts with popular and even folkloristic appeal can be cited.[1]

In this instance, the patron must have been Shah Tahmasp himself, for the designer, project supervisor, and actual painter of many of the miniatures can be identified on grounds of style as Aqa Mirak, one of the shah's major masters and his closest friend among them.[2] Although Shah Tahmasp's disaffection from painting began in the mid-1540s, after the completion of his glorious *Shahnamah* and *Khamsah* of Nizami, it was not until his Edict of Sincere Repentance in 1556 that he foreswore most painting projects in favor of piety and statesmanship. It is not surprising, therefore, that the increasingly religious shah should have wanted a copy of the *Falnamah* illustrated by Aqa Mirak, his artist-friend, who was spared the general withdrawal of patronage.[3]

Aqa Mirak's pictures for this unusually large manuscript are among his boldest compositions, although they lack the subtlety of finish and naturalistic observation of his most sustained pictures for the *Shahnamah* and *Khamsah*.[4] Throughout his career Aqa Mirak, following the practice of other Safavid masters, worked in two modes, one less detailed and less time-consuming than the other. Aqa Mirak's simplified idiom is seen here as well as in the majority of his contributions to Shah Tahmasp's *Shahnamah* and in his two miniatures for the *Haft Awrang* of Jami, done in 1556–1565 and now in the Freer Gallery of Art.[5] It depends for its appeal upon crisply defined areas of immaculate color—delicate and original combinations of off-grays, pinks, rose-violets, and tans, against which he silhouetted intense accents. Perhaps the most inventive designer in the history of Safavid painting, Aqa Mirak enjoyed resolving seemingly impossible compositional challenges. At times it seems as though he began his pictures by casting forms helter-skelter onto the page. Here, however, he began calculatedly, with a symmetrical architectural structure into which he tossed a chaos of dynamic figures, windswept lamps, and the licks of flame from the saint's hand which frighten the royal visitor from the tomb.

The unnerving subject of this remarkable picture must have conformed to the mood of Shah Tahmasp during the 1550s, when he suffered disturbing dreams and intense religiosity. A banner to the right of the spiraling composition is inscribed with an invocation to ʿAli, proof of Shiʿa allegiance. The text on the reverse of the miniature relates to the preceding miniature and to prophecy, exemplifying the nature of the volume. It begins with two couplets:

> When the Prophet Moses threw his stick,
> It became a serpent and devoured the magicians.
> Due to this miracle, he became glorious and great;
> The Creator was pleased with him, and he made the people happy.

The remaining nine lines of text, written in an excellent, clear *taʿliq*, are a rather distant commentary on the couplets.[6]

Shah Tahmasp's and Aqa Mirak's illustrations to the *Falnamah* can be considered influential in the development of Islamic painting. A later version of almost the same size was made at the Ottoman court in a style echoing the spirit and numerous details of the Safavid prototype.[7] One wonders, moreover, if the equally gigantic illustrations on cloth to the Mughal emperor Akbar's *Dastan-i-Amir Hamza* were not inspired by Shah Tahmasp's *Falnamah*, particularly as production of the *Dastan-i-Amir Hamza* was directed by two former members of Tahmasp's atelier who had gone to the Mughal court during the earlier years of the shah's distaste for painting.[8]

S. C. W. and A. W.

1. For instance, the several manuscripts of the *Maqamat* of Hariri produced in various centers in the Near East in the thirteenth and fourteenth centuries and the similarly out-sized *Hamzanamah* commissioned by the Mughal emperor Akbar early in his reign.

2. For a study of Aqa Mirak, see Martin B. Dickson and Stuart C. Welch, *The Houghton Shahnameh* (Cambridge, Mass., 1981), especially 1:95–118.

3. For Shah Tahmasp's changing views toward painting, see Dickson and Welch, *Houghton Shahnameh*, 1:45.

4. Aqa Mirak's style is conveniently found in Stuart C. Welch, *Wonders of the Age* (Cambridge, Mass., 1979), nos. 4, 14, 19, 22, 24, 29, 36, 50, 52, 53, 56, 57, 58, 62.

5. The artist's miniatures for the Freer Jami of 1556–1565 are illustrated in Dickson and Welch, *Houghton Shahnameh*, vol. 1, figs. 163, 164.

6. Translation in Anthony Welch, *Collection*, vol. 3, Ir. M. 65. For other paintings from this same manuscript, see: Ernst Grube, *Muslim Miniature Painting* (Venice, 1962), no. 61 (wrongly ascribed to a series of illustrations to al-Nishapuri's *Lives of the Prophets*); Edwin Binney, 3rd, *Islamic Art from the Collection of Edwin Binney, 3rd* (Washington, D.C., 1966), no. 41; and *The Arts of Islam* (exhib. cat.; London: Hayward Gallery, 1976), no. 612 a, b. It would be possible to reassemble at least a dozen paintings from this fascinating manuscript, which is represented in several public and private collections cited in the publications listed above.

7. See Richard Ettinghausen, *Treasures of Turkey, The Islamic Period* (Lausanne, 1966), p. 203.

8. There is a vast literature on this major Mughal set of paintings. See especially Heinrich Glück, *Die Indischen Miniaturen des Hamsae-Romanes* (Vienna, 1925); Gerhardt Egger, *Hamza-Nama* (Graz, 1974); and Dickson and Welch, *Houghton Shahnameh*.

## 26 / A Manuscript of the Qur'an

Iran; ca. 1550–1570
H. 36.9 cm., W. 24.3 cm.

This manuscript, one of the most splendid of extant Safavid Qur'ans, unfortunately lacks a colophon identifying patron, date, or scribe. But its 328 pages are of such sustained excellence as to imply some princely patron—either Shah Tahmasp (r. 1524–1576) or a connoisseur who, like the shah's nephew Ibrahim Mirza, had access to artists of the highest caliber.

The double-page frontispiece presents verses chosen from the Qur'an for their direct references to the uniqueness of the scripture. In gold cartouches at the top and bottom of each page is written in white *thuluth* four verses from *surah al-Waqi'ah* 56:77–80:

> That this is indeed a noble Qur'an
> In a Book kept hidden
> Which none save the purified,
> A revelation from the Lord of the Worlds.

The gold cartouches are enclosed in dark blue oblongs glittering with thin gold arabesques and small white, red, and yellow flowers; the corners of the oblongs contain crisp white and red arabesques of astonishing beauty. On each page a central large light blue square, enlivened with thin yellow arabesques and red and white flowers, encloses a complex eight-lobed medallion also detailed with arabesques and various flowers. In the center of this sunburst of design is a bold circle inscribed in white *naskh* with a single verse from *surah Bani Isra'il* 17:88:

> Verily, though mankind and the jinn
> should assemble to produce the like
> of this Qur'an, they could not produce
> the like thereof though they were helpers
> one of another.

It is not a standard frontispiece, and the verses must have been selected by a learned theologian.

Overleaf is a second double page, with the complete first *surah* written against a dark blue background filled with arabesques and structured by vertically undulating broad gold bands. Located in the center of each page is the text itself, inscribed in a thin *muhaqqaq*:

> In the name of Allah, the Beneficent,
>   the Merciful.
> Praise be to Allah, Lord of the Worlds,
> The Beneficent, the Merciful.

26 / (also in color)

Owner of the Day of Judgment,
Thee (alone) we worship; Thee (alone) we
  ask for help.
Show us the straight path,
The path of those whom Thou hast favored;
  not the (path) of those who earn Thine
  anger nor of those who go astray.

There are 15 additional full-page illuminations, similarly colored but all highly individual in design, and a smaller illumination around the title of each of the 105 *surahs*. These *surah* headings are inscribed in white *ruq'a* style script. The text itself on the less adorned pages is written in an excellent *naskh*, with twelve lines to the page. The patron for whom the book was made was evidently not a confident Arabist, for beneath the black *naskh* Arabic is an interlinear Persian translation, written in a much smaller red *nasta'liq*.

The manuscript presents a dazzling display of illumination and an equally impressive command of five different script styles.

A. W.

PUBLISHED: Anthony Welch, *Collection,* vol. 2, Ms. 4; Martin Lings and Yasin H. Safadi, *The Qur'an* (London, 1976), no. 133; Alexandra Raeuber, *Islamische Schönschrift* (Zürich: Rietberg Museum, 1979), fig. 28.

## 27 / A Brace of Elegants
Attrib. to Mirza 'Ali
Iran; ca. 1570–1574
(A)  Young Man Reading a Book
    Page and Miniature: H. 14.3 cm., W. 8.1 cm.
(B)  Youth Playing an *Ektar*
    Page: H. 34.4 cm., W. 23.7 cm.
    Miniature: H. 21.7 cm., W. 11.3 cm.

Mirza 'Ali, to whom these romantically precious miniatures can be attributed, was one of the major Safavid artists of the second generation, whose career can be traced from the 1520s to his death in the mid-1570s, a year or so before the death of Shah Tahmasp. Throughout his career certain favorite characterizations were repeated in his pictures. One was a fox-faced bearded man, another a plump youth, and the third the youthful, somewhat epicene dandy found in these two idealized portraits. This young fop is always immaculately dressed and shod, in skintight robe and sleek, pointed vermilion or buff shoes. His changes of appearance provide a history of Safavid thought and taste, for Mirza 'Ali's earlier versions are comparatively earthy, even stolid, as in the miniatures for Shah Tahmasp's

**27A** / Young man reading a book

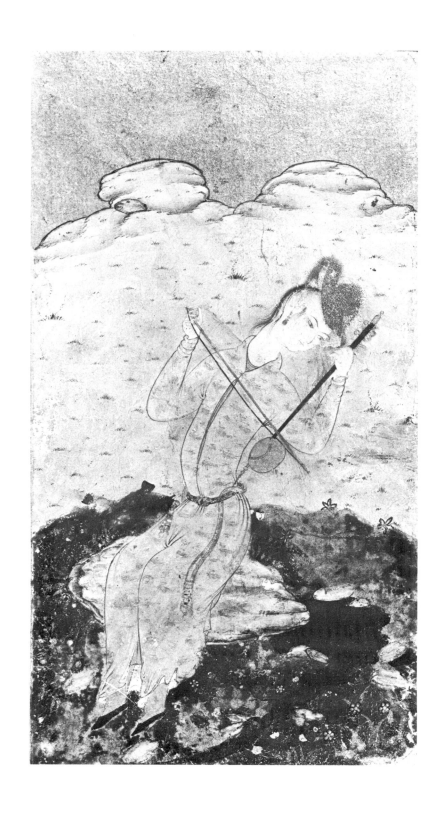

**27B** / Youth playing an *ektar*

*Shahnamah,* painted in the 1520s and 1530s.[1] During the more classical years represented by the British Library *Khamsah* (Quintet) of Nizami, dated to 1539–1543, this lean young man became more credible, with true-to-life proportions and portrait-like features. Nevertheless, his appearances in the Quintet's elevatedly fashionable court scenes reveal manneristic tendencies. His neck begins to resemble a cone, his face and torso are feline, with a sinuous litheness that brings to mind Pontormo's Italian equivalents.

These suggestive characteristics become more extreme with the passage of time. When, following the shah's Edict of Sincere Repentance in 1556, Mirza 'Ali began working for the shah's nephew and son-in-law, Sultan Ibrahim Mirza, the vogue for expressive distortion of form took hold, whipped along by the extravagant young patron's radical tastes. As time passed, the near-classicism admired by Shah Tahmasp gave way to wildness; this progression can be seen in the miniatures of the Freer Gallery's 1556–1565 *Haft Awrang* of Jami if we compare those painted in the 1550s with others created when the project neared its end.[2]

In 1565 Shah Tahmasp turned against his erstwhile young favorite, son-in-law, and nephew, whose keen patronage of painting had given him vicarious pleasure. Sultan Ibrahim was exiled to Qa'in, a small oasis in Kuhistan, where he was nominally governor, under sorely reduced circumstances. Later he was sent to Sabzivar, where he remained from 1567 to 1574. A few painters, fortunately, continued to serve him; and in 1565 much of his time was spent at Herat where, indeed, the colophon of "Layla and Majnun" (one of the seven books of the *Haft Awrang*) was written. Nevertheless, the deprived Sultan Ibrahim is said to have consoled himself with pious acts; and the works of two particularly devoted artists who continued to serve him betray moods of nostalgic longing. Along with the more aggressive Shaykh Muhammad, who served his saddened master as a virtual artistic alter ego, Mirza 'Ali provided consolation during these bleak times.

Mirza 'Ali's *Young Man Reading a Book* must have brought moments of pleasure, even at Sabzivar. The courtly young man sits trim, limber, and erect, yet seems as sweetly vulnerable as the poppy drooping under its own weight in his turban. As always, however, Mirza 'Ali's figure is anatomically convincing, with each bone, sinew, and muscle logically portrayed and, in this instance, lending flexibility and implying stamina. Inasmuch as Sultan Ibrahim Mirza survived his exile and returned to the shah's favor at Qazvin, where he was appointed to high office in 1574, one might consider Mirza 'Ali's characterization significant of good times ahead. In the meantime, too, the lad's spirits seem to have been buoyed by the reading of love verses.

The same artist's *Young Man Playing an Ektar,* however, stresses the loneliness of exile. As he bows the strings in a bleak, rocky landscape, one senses the piercing music in which he is lost. The bleak mood is intensified when we know that soon after Shah Tahmasp died in 1576 Sultan Ibrahim Mirza was murdered.

Were these mysterious youths painted as actual portraits? Or do they represent flower-like metaphors for divine love? Both interpretations, we suspect, were intended.

S. C. W.

1. For Mirza ʿAli's artistic personality, career, and works, see Martin B. Dickson and Stuart C. Welch, *The Houghton Shahnameh* (Cambridge, Mass., 1981), 1:129–53; Stuart C. Welch, *Persian Painting* (New York, 1976); and idem, *Wonders of the Age* (Cambridge, Mass., 1979), nos. 7, 26, 28, 38, 54, 59, 69, 70, 78, 82, 83, 85.

2. The Freer *Haft Awrang* of Jami is discussed at length in Dickson and Welch, *Houghton Shahnameh*, where Sultan Ibrahim Mirza's life, character, and patronage are fully documented and illustrated.

PUBLISHED: Anthony Welch, *Collection,* vol. 3, Ir. M. 71; Dickson and Welch, *Houghton Shahnameh,* vol. 1, fig. 208.

## 28 / Young Man in a Gold Hat

Iran, Qazvin; ca. 1587
Page: H. 36 cm., W. 23 cm.
Miniature: H. 13.7 cm., W. 8.7 cm.

A young man kneels on his right knee and rests his hands on his left thigh while he looks into the distance. Four long tresses of hair trail down his arms; his gold hat is elegantly turned up at the sides. His collar and buttons are gold too, and his belt and hanging sash are tinted light blue and red. His garment falls in graceful swirls over his right leg, and the extra long, tight sleeves are softly gathered above his wrists. In the upper left is an owner's seal: "'Abbas, the servant of the King of Holiness."[1] It is the standard seal of Shah ʿAbbas I (r. 1587–1629), and the drawing probably entered the royal library about 1587. The drawing is bordered by a number of inscriptions that do not refer to patron or artist but may refer obliquely to subject.

The two vertical lines at the right are a Safavid poem:

> A man who becomes acquainted with desire
> Eventually falls into poverty.

Under the youth's feet are two lines of Chaghatai Turkish from the works of Mir ʿAli Shir Nawaʾi, the poet and *vazir* at the court of Sultan Husayn Bayqara in late fifteenth-century Herat. At the bottom of the page are two lines from the works of the Persian poet Saʿdi:

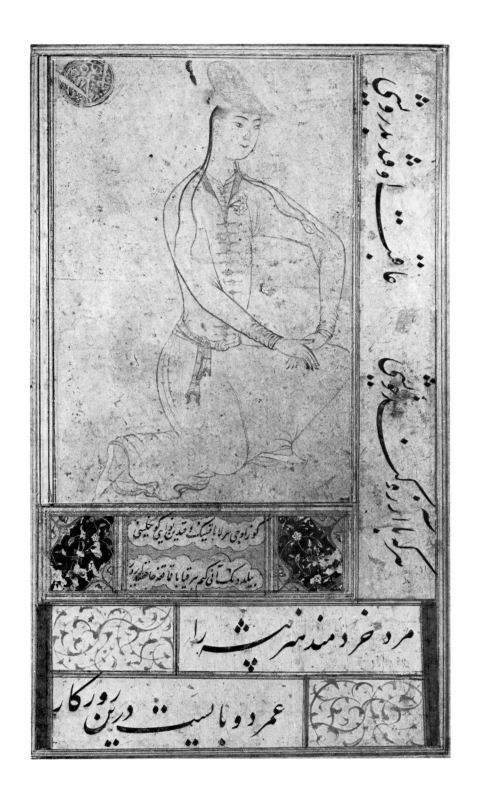

A wise and artful man must have
Two lives in this world . . .[2]

On the reverse are verses from Firdausi's *Shahnamah*, presumably appended when the drawing became part of a royal album.

The drawing is strikingly similar to a dated work by the young master Riza, who became the leading painter at the court of Shah ʿAbbas.[3]

A. W.

1. The title "King of Holiness" refers to ʿAli, the great saintly figure of Shiʿa Islam.
2. The lines are completed as follows: "So that with one he can gather experiences / And with the other bring these experiences into action."
3. Reproduced in O. F. Akimushkin and A. A. Ivanov, *Persidskie miniaturi XIV–XVII v.* (Moscow, 1968), fig. 61.

PUBLISHED: Anthony Welch, *Collection*, vol. 3, Ir. M. 73.

## 29 / Two Pages from a *Shahnamah* for Shah Ismaʿil II

Iran, Qazvin; 1576–1577
(A) Rustam Kills a Dragon
  By Sadiqi
  Page: H. 43 cm., W. 31 cm.
(B) Isfandiyar Kills the *Simurgh*
  By Siyavush
  Page: H. 40.5 cm., W. 29.7 cm.

Like his father, Shah Tahmasp, whom he succeeded in 1576, Shah Ismaʿil II (r. 1576–1577) commissioned a *Shahnamah* of substantial size and quality on his accession. The reign of this mentally unstable monarch lasted less than two years, and the manuscript was left uncompleted. Its pages, now dispersed, are in many collections.[1] Despite the brevity of his reign, Ismaʿil II managed to assemble in Qazvin a fine atelier comprising third-generation Safavid painters, many of them undoubtedly trained by masters like Mirza ʿAli and Muzaffar ʿAli. Most of the surviving illustrated pages are inscribed with painters' names: these ascriptions are all in the same hand, presumably that of the shah's librarian or perhaps the director of the *Shahnamah* project. Two painters, Sadiqi Bek and Siyavush, were evidently more esteemed than their colleagues, for together they were responsible for a large majority of the illustrations.

In a lively miniature by Sadiqi, a gold and black dragon has burst out of a mass of rocks, some of them transformed into small faces upturned in astonishment, but Rustam has not been taken by surprise. While his horse bites into the dragon's spine, the hero chops off its head with a mighty

**29A** / Rustam kills a dragon

**29B** / Isfandiyar kills the *simurgh* (also in color)

blow. Below a singing bird at the left appears the artist's name. Although the iconography of the scene is traditional, the painter has rendered it with impressive energy and dramatic color.

About Sadiqi much is known, for he was a prolific writer as well as painter. Besides his many poems, he left two lengthy literary works of fundamental importance to Safavid art history. His *Tazkirah-yi Majma' al-Khawass* (An Account of an Assembly of Worthies) is a frequently acrimonious account of the patrons, poets, painters, and miscellaneous men of culture he knew during his long and often embattled career.[2] The *Qanun al-Suvar (Canons of Art)* is a poetical treatise on the techniques of traditional Persian painting.[3] Together, the two books provide enough information about Sadiqi's personal life so that a plausible biography can be constructed. Born about 1533, he initially took up the military career traditional in his family, then abandoned it to become a painter and man of letters. About 1568, after three years' study of calligraphy, he became a student of painting under Muzaffar 'Ali, one of the most eminent contemporary painters, and by 1576 he was awarded his important role in the Shahnamah project for the new king. Some time after Shah 'Abbas I took the throne in 1587, Sadiqi was appointed director of the royal library, in which post he so prospered that by 1593 he could commission his own precious manuscript, an *Anvar-i Suhayli* lavishly and imaginatively illustrated by himself.[4] During this period he also oversaw the production of a great *Shahnamah* for the new monarch,[5] but this manuscript, like Shah Isma'il II's, was never finished, perhaps because Sadiqi's overbearing personality and high-handed dealings (he stole from the royal library and subsequently sold one of Bihzad's masterpieces) finally led to his dismissal in 1596–1597. During his remaining years Sadiqi continued active, executing a few fine drawings and completing his various literary works.[6]

Not all *simurghs* were benevolent birds; one of the more evil sort is confronted in another miniature from the *Shahnamah* by the Iranian hero Isfandiyar in a chariot armed with projecting spikes. Defending its nest and two chicks in the massive tree at the left, the *simurgh* impales itself on Isfandiyar's vehicle. The hero's white horse ignores the frenzied death above it, while Isfandiyar and his warriors look on unmoved.

Brilliant in composition and color, this picture is Siyavush's finest work of art and is one of the great paintings of late-sixteenth-century Iran. The master's name is written at the lower left. Siyavush served as a page to Shah Tahmasp in the late 1530s, and it was Tahmasp's perception of his talent that led him to study painting, eventually becoming, like Sadiqi, a student of Muzaffar 'Ali. Like his colleague, Siyavush only emerged as a master in his own right with the *Shahnamah* commissioned by Isma'il II in 1576–1577, for which he provided at least thirteen illustrations, more than any other painter. After the death of Isma'il II he worked for various patrons and enjoyed the support of 'Abbas I, for whom he seems only to have provided drawings. He retired to Shiraz in the last years of the sixteenth century and died some time between 1606 and 1616.[7]

A. W.

1. The unfinished manuscript was apparently dismembered by the dealer Demotte some time after 1912. A total of eight pages (with nine miniatures) are in Prince Sadruddin's collection (Ir. M. 29–29/B; Ir. M. 69–69/D), and they bear the names of six masters: Sadiqi, Siyavush, Naqdi, Burji, Mihrab, and Murad. Three other painters are known to have worked on this *Shahnamah*: 'Ali 'Asghar (the father of Riza), Zayn al-'Abidin, and 'Abdullah Shirazi. For further discussion of the *Shahnamah* made for Isma'il II, see Basil W. Robinson, "Isma'il II's Copy of the *Shahnamah*," *Iran, Journal of the British Institute of Persian Studies* 14 (1976): 1–8; and Anthony Welch, *Artists for the Shah* (New Haven and London, 1976).

2. Sadiqi Bek, *Majma' al-Khawass*, intro. and trans. from Chaghatai Turkish into Persian by A. R. Khayyampur (Tabriz, 1948). The *Majma' al-Khawass* is discussed in T. Gandjei, "Notes on the Life and Work of Sadiqi: A Poet and Painter of Safavid Times," *Der Islam* 52 (no. 1, 1975); and in Welch, *Artists for the Shah*, who is indebted to Martin B. Dickson for first drawing his attention to it.

3. Sadiqi Bek, *Qanun al-Suvar*, ed. A. U. Kaziev (Baku, 1963). A complete English translation of this important treatise appears in Martin B. Dickson and Stuart C. Welch, *The Houghton Shahnameh* (Cambridge, Mass., 1981).

4. See cat. no. 32.

5. Unfortunately all that remains of the unfinished *Shahnamah* made for Shah 'Abbas I ca. 1587–1595 are fourteen miniatures in the Chester Beatty Library, Dublin. See A. J. Arberry, Basil W. Robinson, E. Blochet, and J. V. S. Wilkinson, *The Chester Beatty Library, Dublin: a Catalogue of the Persian Manuscripts and Miniatures* (Dublin, 1962), vol. 3, Ms. 277; and Welch, *Artists for the Shah*.

6. For further biographical and literary information concerning Sadiqi, see Dickson and Welch, *The Houghton Shahnameh*; Welch, *Artists for the Shah*; and Gandjei, "Notes on the Life and Work of Sadiqi: A Poet and Painter of Safavid Times."

7. For Siyavush's life and career, see Welch, *Artists for the Shah*.

PUBLISHED: (A and B) Robinson, "Isma'il II's Copy of the Shahnama," nos. 20 and 48 and pl. 4; Basil W. Robinson et al., *Persian and Mughal Art* (London, 1976), nos. 19x, 19xxi; Welch, *Artists for the Shah*, pp. 25, 201, and fig. 2; (B) G. Marteau and H. Vever, *Miniatures persanes exposées au Musée des Arts Décoratifs*, 2 vols. (Paris, 1912), pl. 104 and fig. 128.

## 30 / A Manuscript of the *Diwan* of Ibrahim Mirza

Iran; 1582
H. 24.7 cm., W. 17.1 cm.

Born in 1543–1544, Ibrahim Mirza was the son of Bahram Mirza, brother of Shah Tahmasp (r. 1524–1576). Both father and uncle set models of connoisseurship and artistic patronage for the young prince, who became while still very young one of the most appealing and fascinating figures in the history of Safavid art. Like all Safavid princes, he was given training in calligraphy and painting, but he also proved adept in other endeavors, so that Qadi Ahmad, who served under him, praised him twenty years after his death for his abilities in music, the sciences, poetry, cooking, sports,

**30** / folio 23b: Ibrahim Mirza's garden party (also in color)

and crafts.¹ Bahram Mirza had died when Ibrahim was only six, and the orphaned prince grew up under the aegis of his uncle the shah. In 1555–1556 (A.H. 963) this poet-artist-scholar was married to the shah's daughter, Gauhar-sultan, and appointed to the prestigious governorship of Mashhad in eastern Iran. His relationship with his supicious and unpredictable uncle was often difficult, but Ibrahim assembled in Mashhad a brilliant court to which he attracted many of Iran's finest artistic talents who had been left masterless when Tahmasp foreswore the arts. The single most important surviving achievement of those years was the great 1556–1565 *Haft Awrang* of Jami, copied by five of Iran's leading scribes and illustrated by six of its greatest painters, masters who had previously painted for Shah Tahmasp.² A great *muraqqa* (album) that Qadi Ahmad describes may have been equally splendid: "In Holy Mashhad [Ibrahim Mirza] put together an album of the writings of masters and paintings of Maulana Behzad [Bihzad] and others. It was completed with the help of rare masters, skillful craftsmen, incomparable experts in writing, and peerless calligraphers. Indeed, such an arrangement was made and such an album showed its face, that every page of it was worthy of a hundred praises. . . ."³

In 1574 Ibrahim Mirza returned to Qazvin, where he remained for the last few years of his life. When the old shah died in 1576, Ibrahim was serving him as grand master of ceremonies and was presumably still active as a patron. His library numbered over three thousand volumes, and his own poetry, written under the pen-name Jahi (the Glorious), included some five thousand verses in Turkish and Persian. He had also become a practitioner of calligraphy and connoisseur of Mir 'Ali al-Katib's *nasta'liq* style of script and had collected several albums of his work.

Shah Tahmasp's unstable son, Isma'il II, became shah in 1576 after a bitter and bloody struggle within the royal house. He ruled for only a year and a half, during which he succeeded in executing most of the Safavid family. Although Ibrahim Mirza had kept his distance from the feuds and had tried to avoid antagonizing his cousin, he was murdered on 24 February 1577. In her grief his wife washed clean the pages of her husband's marvellous *muraqqa* so that it could not be appropriated by Isma'il II; she died soon afterward. Their daughter, Gauhar-shad, arranged that her parents be buried in Mashhad, and in tribute to his beloved master Qadi Ahmad collected three thousand of the prince's verses and wrote a preface for them.⁴ His edition seems not to have survived, and until now Ibrahim's poetry has been known only through the few passages quoted by Qadi Ahmad in his treatise on painters and calligraphers.

According to the preface to this manuscript of Ibrahim's *Diwan*, it was compiled by Ibrahim's daughter—presumably Gauhar-shad—who gave the pious duty of copying and illustrating it to the finest calligraphers and painters of her day. It is not as extensive as Qadi Ahmad's reported edition, for the book contains only eighty-eight pages, with nine lines or less of text to the page. It is bound in a handsome gold-stamped late sixteenth-century binding; the margins of each page are illuminated in gold, and there are several handsome 'unwans (chapter-title illuminations) as well as a brilliantly decorated double-page frontispiece. The prince's Persian poetry occupies the first sixty-eight pages, and his Turkish poems fill the last twenty. Though he was a competent poet, Ibrahim's poetry does not perhaps deserve the elaborate praise that Qadi Ahmad lavished on it. The princess knew her father's penchant for Mir 'Ali's calligraphy, and she commissioned a scribe, unfortunately not identified, who was a follower of that great master's style.

The book's six single-page and one double-page illustrations were painted by several different masters who had either been trained by or known the work of Mirza 'Ali, one of the prince's favorite painters.[5] Only one of them, however, is identified: in the lower left of folio 23a is a rock, minutely inscribed: "On this stone the painter has written that this humble world lacks constancy. Therefore be happy. Work of 'Abdullah al-Mudhahhib in the year 990."

Qadi Ahmad was well acquainted with the life and work of 'Abdullah al-Mudhahhib (the Gilder):

> Maulana 'Abdullah Mudhahhib, who was a native of Shiraz, was highly skilled in ornamental gilding and in drawing frontispieces and shamsas. None worked better than he in preparing oil colors. For twenty years he was employed in the kitabkhanah [library] of Prince Abu'l-Fath Sultan Ibrahim Mirza; he was a courtier and drew a salary. After the demise of that exalted Highness, he left the court service and having settled down in Holy Mashhad, took up the duties of a carpet spreader at the sanctuary and attendant at the grave of the above-mentioned Prince.[6]

It would seem that he produced only one illustration for Ibrahim's Diwan, and it is his only signed painting, but it is reasonable to assume that, as a famous gilder and illuminator, he decorated the book's margins and provided its sumptuous frontispiece and 'unwans. Although Qadi Ahmad speaks of the painter's loyal retirement to a humble post in 1577, he apparently first worked briefly for Ibrahim's murderer, Isma'il II, for a second chronicler, Iskandar Munshi, wrote in 1616: "Maulana 'Abdullah Shirazi was also an accomplished worker in gold; after the murder of Sultan Ibrahim Mirza, Isma'il Mirza gave him an appointment in the library."[7]

Even after Isma'il II's death, 'Abdullah's retirement was not complete, for in 1582 he was working for Gauhar-shad to produce this manuscript honoring her father. Stylistically, the book's script, illumination, and illustration are all derived from the 1556–1565 Haft Awrang, the great achievement of Ibrahim's patronage. His daughter evidently intended that this copy of his *Diwan* should not only preserve her father's poetry but should also remain a testimony to his taste.

A. W.

1. See Qadi Ahmad, *Calligraphers and Painters*, trans. from the Persian by Vladimir Minorsky (Washington, D.C., 1959), pp. 2–14, 153–67, 183–84. The following account of Ibrahim Mirza relies heavily on three studies: Stuart C. Welch, *A King's Book of Kings* (New York, 1972); idem, *Persian Painting* (New York, 1976); and Martin B. Dickson and Stuart C. Welch, *The Houghton Shahnameh* (Cambridge, Mass., 1981).
2. For an identification of these painters, see Welch, *Persian Painting*, and Dickson and Welch, *Houghton Shahnameh*.
3. Qadi Ahmad, *Calligraphers and Painters*, p. 183.
4. Qadi Ahmad, *Calligraphers and Painters*, p. 157n.
5. For Mirza 'Ali, see cat. no. 27.
6. Qadi Ahmad, *Calligraphers and Painters*, pp. 189–90.
7. Quoted and trans. T. W. Arnold, *Painting in Islam* (Oxford, 1928; New York, 1965), p. 144. For a study of the patronage of Isma'il II, see Anthony Welch, *Artists for the Shah* (New Haven and London, 1976).

PUBLISHED: G. Marteau and H. Vever, *Miniatures persanes exposées au Musée des Arts Décoratifs*, 2 vols. (Paris, 1912).

## 31 / Attacked by a Dragon

Attrib. to Sadiqi Bek
Iran, Qazvin; ca. 1590–1595
Page: H. 31.7 cm., W. 21.1 cm.
Miniature: H. 17.6 cm., W. 12.3 cm.

Dragon attacks are a common subject in Islamic art, though the reason for their popularity and the possible underlying significance of the theme are not yet known. They appear frequently in illustrated manuscripts of the *Shahnamah,* the *Darabnamah,* and similar epics,[1] and are not uncommon among Iranian single-page drawings of the late sixteenth and the seventeenth centuries.

Thus the scene of a ravening dragon rushing down from a rocky height to attack a man on horseback has a well-established iconography. But for all its thematic familiarity, this drawing is unusual in its sparseness of detail: it offers just enough information to establish the basic composition and theme and is characterized by a kind of pictorial parsimony. Whereas dragons usually rush down from craggy heights, we have here only two faint stones under the beast's left hind foot and no indication of the ground on which it stands. Horse and rider, likewise, are set in a mere nondescript hint of landscape: a large and a small rock and a fanlike spread of broad leaves. At the far right, a faintly sketched camel's head may imply that the horseman is leading a caravan. The reactions depicted are equally unexpected: the plump horse looks slightly anxious but is not shying away from

what is presumably a sudden and dangerous assault; the equally portly rider has not drawn knife or sword but is regarding the dragon's tail with the equanimity of a rather bored naturalist. This, therefore, is not a simple drawing of a familiar subject but one filled with interesting innuendo.

Although this understated and subtly humorous drawing is not signed, it can confidently be attributed to Sadiqi Bek, one of the master draftsmen and painters of late sixteenth-century Iran.[2] When he completed this drawing, he must have been about sixty years old, and his art at this time is characterized by lengthy, knife-sharp calligraphic strokes, running gradually from thick to thin and avoiding shading lest it weaken the purity of the stroke or evoke too much sense of body or of warmth. He tends toward the abstract and cerebral rather than the sensual, and as this fine drawing indicates, he can treat a shopworn theme with iconoclastic freshness.

A. W.

1. For a Safavid rendering of a dragon attack, see the page from the Houghton *Shahnamah* illustrated in Stuart C. Welch, *Persian Painting* (New York, 1976), pl. 9. For a Mughal miniature of a dragon swallowing an unfortunate monarch, see a page from a Mughal *Darabnamah* illustrated in idem, *Imperial Mughal Painting* (New York, 1978), pl. 5.

2. For an examination of the life and career of Sadiqi Bek, see Anthony Welch, *Artists for the Shah* (New Haven and London, 1976), chaps. 3, 4.

PUBLISHED: Frederick R. Martin, *The Miniature Paintings and Painters of Persia, India, and Turkey* (London, 1912), vol. 2, pl. 93; Welch, *Artists for the Shah*, pl. 28; idem, *Collection*, vol. 3, Ir. M. 75.

## 32 / A Manuscript of the *Anvar-i Suhayli*

Iran, Qazvin; 1593
H. 30 cm., W. 21 cm.

The Sanskrit *Tales of Bidpai* were moralizing animal fables first translated into Pahlavi, then into Arabic (under the title *Kalila wa Dimna*), and subsequently into Persian. The *Anvar-i Suhayli* (Lights of Canopus) is a version composed in verbose and florid Persian prose by Husayn Waʿiz-i Kashifi at the late fifteenth-century court of the Timurid ruler in Herat, Sultan Husayn Bayqara. The book continued popular in Safavid Iran, and must have been a favorite of the poet, painter, chronicler, and courtier Sadiqi Bek, who took the unprecedented step of commissioning a manuscript of it for himself.

Sadiqi's appointment as *kitabdar* (director of the royal library) by Shah ʿAbbas I about 1587 had made him virtual head of the Safavi artistic hierarchy and must have brought him significant income as well as stature and authority. In his numerous writings Sadiqi reveals himself as proud, opinionated, and generally disagreeable, and he was apparently neither an

**32** / folio 22a: Bazindah and the sudden storm (also in color)

**32** / folio 139b: The pigeons snared

شعلهٔ آتش دوی بجانب ماه داده شد ونیز می آید می میمون کشت ای ستمکاران
دلاز ار این بیابان اجل وآن که می آید بیک مرک دل خوش دارید که آگر هزار
جان دارید یکی نهید وحالی که سموم برسد شما را هم خاکستر سازد وبآتش
بیدادی که دردهاد بوزنگان زنده بسوزی ایشان در این سخن بودند که گفت
سموم برسید ومیموز ابا جماعت شاه

وسپاه حسان برجای ببسوخت وبگر
از ایشان از ان بیابان بیرون نیامدند وملک بوزنگان با لشکر خود بجزیره آمد
پیشه را حالی دیدند وملک از نکو دت اعیان صافی نظر
بگفت شام منکت وصبح ظفر دمید که شبخوان رنج بهار طرب رسید

32 / folio 198a: The apes' revenge

easy nor an effective supervisor, for in 1596–1597 the shah dismissed him, though continuing to pay him his full salary until his death about 1612.[1]

Sadiqi commissioned his manuscript about midway in his decade-long career as *kitabdar*. The book's informative colophon provides the following information:

> Copied by ibn Na'im Muhammad al-Husayni al-Tabrizi (may forgiveness come to him!) on the thirteenth day of the month. It is well and victoriously completed in Safar of the year 1002. It is written as it is ordered by the rare man of the time, the second Mani and the Bihzad of the age, Sadiqi Musavvir.

The date corresponds to 8 November 1593. Nothing is known of the calligrapher, and there is no mention of any other patron. Annemarie Schimmel has noted that the text is written in the *naskh* style rather than in the *nasta'liq* one would expect in this period. Had Sadiqi ordered or intended the manuscript for someone else, presumably that person would have been named and Sadiqi would not have allowed himself to be praised in such fulsome and patron-like terms. On the front flyleaf is a note indicating that by June 1618 the manuscript had come into the possession of an Indian aristocrat; it had probably been sold soon after Sadiqi's death.

The book's 365 pages are bound in a contemporary lacquer binding of the highest quality: over a green background course arabesques in red, black, and gold. The 107 miniatures are all by the same hand, and although none is signed, stylistic evidence indicates that they are Sadiqi's work. Pigments tend to be thinner and less lavish than in either the 1576–1577 *Shahnamah* or the *Shahnamah* of circa 1587–1597,[2] perhaps because Sadiqi was paying for this *Anvar-i Suhayli* himself. But the pictures are also more radical than those he did for royal patrons, and one can surmise that his strongly independent personality responded to the artistic freedom of working completely according to his own taste.[3] Subject matter is frequently striking for its departure from conventional iconography: interiors of humble peasant dwellings and fly-infested markets are shown, and animals and outdoor settings are rendered with a naturalism, drama, and attention to movement more indicative of Sadiqi's own interests than of court aesthetics. As a result, the manuscript is not only one of the most impressive works of Safavid painting but also a prime source of information about one of Iran's most distinguished and individualistic artists.

Folio 22a (*Bazindah and the Sudden Storm*) illustrates the first story in Book 1 of the *Anvar-i Suhayli*.[4] Two pigeons, long resident together, differed about the value of travel. Nawazindah was a homebody, afraid of leaving the nest; Bazindah was more daring and longed to see the world. After much discussion he left and in a short while reached a beautiful meadow at the foot of a mountain, but he had scarcely enjoyed its beauties when a sudden storm swept down on him. Sadiqi also illustrated subsequent tribulations of the hapless bird, but this miniature is one of the most powerful renderings of wind, storm, and lightning in Iranian art.

The first story of Book 3 is a tale of guidance offered and rejected. A flock of hungry pigeons ignores the wise warning of its leader, and on folio 139b (*The Pigeons Snared*) Sadiqi illustrates their capture by a fowler. Warfare and righteous victory are the subject of the eleventh story of Book 4, in which a band of apes, earlier attacked and plundered by an army of bears, is revenged by its *vazir* Maimun, who poses as a traitor and lures the bears into a fiery desert where they, along with Maimun, are destroyed. Sadiqi's illustration, fol. 198a (*The Apes' Revenge*), shows the heroic Maimun at the right and the five bears to the left, all dying in the heat of the desert.

A. W.

1. For further information on Sadiqi, see Anthony Welch, *Artists for the Shah* (New Haven and London, 1976), pp. 41–149. I am profoundly grateful to Martin B. Dickson of Princeton University, who first pointed out to me the existence and importance of Sadiqi's literary works. Dickson's translation of Sadiqi's treatise *Qanun al-Suvar* has been published in Martin B. Dickson and Stuart C. Welch, *The Houghton Shahnameh* (Cambridge, Mass., 1981).

2. See cat. no. 29.

3. For other works by Sadiqi, see cat. nos. 29, 31, and 33.

4. For an English translation, see Arthur N. Wollaston, trans., *The Anwar-i Suhaili or Lights of Canopus* (London: 1877).

PUBLISHED: Basil W. Robinson, "Two Persian Manuscripts in the Library of the Marquess of Bute," *Oriental Art*, Spring, 1974; Welch, *Artists for the Shah*, pp. 125–43; *The Arts of Islam* (exhib. cat.; London: Hayward Gallery, 1976), no. 621.

## 33 / A Seated Youth

Attrib. to Sadiqi Bek
Iran, Qazvin or Isfahan; ca. 1595–1600
Page: H. 35.7 cm., W. 23.2 cm.
Miniature: H. 18.6 cm., W. 12.4 cm.

The subject is one of the most common in later Safavid art: a well-fed and elegantly dressed youth gazing at a point beyond our own perceptions. From the dragon-like clouds to the broad-leafed plants and plump fruits, the landscape is filled with predictable conventions. It was the manipulation of these almost iconic elements that tested the ability of an artist, and those who excelled in their use during the reign of Shah 'Abbas I (r. 1587–1629) were Sadiqi and Riza, the former a senior and well-established master, the latter a gifted prodigy whose art shaped the style and direction

of much subsequent Safavid painting and drawing.[1] Despite Sadiqi's great-er age and experience, his later work, of which this brilliantly rendered stereotype of ideal beauty is an excellent example, owes much to Riza's predilection for calligraphic line and winsome elegance. Though it does not bear Sadiqi's name, this drawing has a linear incisiveness, a predilection for sharp edges, a certain chilly distance in the slightly pudgy face, that mark it as his work. Like many objects of this sort in Islamic art, its beauty was necessary to its function, for the couplet at the top indicates that it was intended to secure a blessing on its owner:

> O, you branch of spring, how nicely you sway.
> May the torment of time (and wind) never upset you.[2]

The springtime setting and the youth in the spring of his years are change-less and eternal.

A. W.

1. For the relationship between Sadiqi and Riza, see Anthony Welch, *Artists for the Shah* (New Haven and London, 1976).
2. I am grateful to Annemarie Schimmel for this translation.

## 34 / Page Boy with Bottle and Cup

By Riza-yi ʿAbbasi
Iran, Isfahan; 1625
Page: H. 30.8 cm., W. 20.1 cm.
Miniature: H. 18.9 cm., W. 9.2 cm.

Although the prevailing heroic and literary subject matter of Iranian painting from the fourteenth through sixteenth centuries did not entirely disappear in the seventeenth century, Safavid painting from about 1600 to 1722 was dominated by different images. Among the most important of these was the solitary youth, usually male and invariably elegant, affluent, and beautiful, at least in seventeenth-century Iranian terms. They are posed in languid inaction, their attention not inwardly focused but wistfully wandering toward an unspecified distant point. This masterful painting perfectly expresses the type. Its maker, Riza-yi ʿAbbasi, clearly owed much to earlier artists like Mirza ʿAli and Shaykh Muhammad, but he developed the image with such fluency and to such a pitch of grace that it became a kind of icon in seventeenth-century painting in Iran.[1]

The young man looks absentmindedly to the left. Against his green shirt he holds a gold bottle, and a small ceramic cup hangs limply from his

**34** / (also in color)

delicate left hand. Gold trims his purple coat and broad blue sash, and his brilliant yellow trousers are decorated with green and gold birds, lavender clouds, and green plants. His blue hat is trimmed with brown fur, and, like his whole attire, must have been in the latest mode.

Much is known about the artist, Riza. He came to the court of Shah 'Abbas I soon after that ruler's accession in 1587 and flourished there as an illustrator of manuscripts and a painter and draftsman of album pages until about 1605, when, according to reliable literary sources, he experienced a sudden metamorphosis, largely gave up his profession, and took to spending his time with wrestlers and persons of ill repute. For the period from 1605 to 1615 we have few pictures that can be reliably attributed to Riza, and this lack supports the disapproving accounts of his chroniclers. But from 1615 until his death in 1635 Riza returned to his former profession with renewed vigor, probably revivified by his long leave of absence and certainly filled with new observations and experiences, for his later drawings show an artist whose subject matter goes beyond stereotyped court images to record many other social strata.[2]

This courtly picture was most probably made for the royal patron, Shah 'Abbas, who deeply admired Riza's work and had tolerantly put up with the artist's decade-long truancy. The inscription at the lower left informs us that the drawing was completed in the month of rabi' al-awwal in the year 1034 (December 1624–January 1625) by the most humble Riza-yi 'Abbasi.

In the last two decades of his life after his return to painting, Riza was also a brilliant teacher, and he so developed the talents of his finest students that they emerged as distinctly individual artists. Some, like Muhammad Qasim and Muhammad Yusuf, tended to follow the courtly vein in Riza's later art.[3] Riza's son Shafi' 'Abbasi, however, turned toward sensitive studies of flora and fauna and became a gifted designer of textiles.[4] Mu'in Musavvir, surely Riza's greatest student, moved from court images to witty or documentary scenes of daily life with equal ease and talent.[5] It testifies to Riza's genius that he could foster the genius in others and in doing so establish himself as the guiding spirit of seventeenth-century figural art in Iran.

A. W.

1. For Riza's role in this regard, see Anthony Welch, *Artists for the Shah* (New Haven and London, 1976); and idem, "Painting and Patronage under Shah 'Abbas," in *Studies on Isfahan, Iranian Studies*, 1974, pp. 458–508.

2. For a selection of Riza's works and an examination of his career, see Anthony Welch, *Shah 'Abbas and the Arts of Isfahan* (New York, 1973), nos. 6–12, 50, 51, and p. 147. For Mu'in's sensitive portrait of Riza, see ibid., no. 76.

3. See cat. no 35.

4. See Welch, *Shah 'Abbas and the Arts of Isfahan*, no. 58.

5. See cat. no. 39.

## 35 / A Display of Verse

By Muhammad Qasim Musavvir
Iran, Isfahan; ca. 1650
Page: H. 33.4 cm., W. 23.5 cm.
Miniature: H. 19.9 cm., W. 13.1 cm.

The long white sheet of paper with four diagonal lines of poetry in *nasta'liq* script is the focus of attention:

> May the world fulfill your wishes
>   from three lips—
> The lips of the beloved, the lips of
>   a stream, and the lips of a cup.
> May you remain in this world so long
> That you pray on the grave of the firmament.

The final, horizontal, line gives the name of the calligrapher and the painter of the whole picture: "The humblest of the worshipful slaves, Muhammad Qasim Musavvir." Since the sheet's upper right contains the single word "He," referring to God, the artist's obeisance is probably being offered both to Allah and to his royal patron, Shah 'Abbas II (r. 1642–1666).

The conceit of the "three lips" is not uncommon in Iranian poetry: it equates various kinds of love (for the earthly and the divine beloved, for natural beauty, and for wine); and though the wine cup, so often shown in later Safavid paintings, is omitted here, the stream and the human beloved are present and bring this painting closer than most seventeenth-century album pages to traditional literary illustration.

Isfahan painting under the aegis of Shah 'Abbas II and (presumably) other highly placed patrons was diverse, but most of its main currents had been introduced in Riza's work, and it was his students and followers who dominated the figural arts. Muhammad Qasim was among the most gifted of these, and some of his finest pictures portray this well-established type—the idle, ideal beauty in a stance of affluent grace.

On the reverse of this album page is fine calligraphy in the *ta'liq* style of script. Six lines present one of the *Hadith* (Traditional Sayings) of the Prophet; the remaining three state that it was written in Qazvin in 1563–1564 (A.H. 971) by the artist 'Ali al-Mashhadi on the order of Nur al-Din Mashhadi. The scribe cannot be identified with the great master Sultan 'Ali Mashhadi who died in 1520 (A.H. 926).

A. W.

PUBLISHED: Laurence Binyon, J. V. S. Wilkinson, and Basil Gray, *Persian Miniature Painting* (London, 1933), no. 294; Phyllis Ackerman, *Guide to the Exhibition of Persian Art* (New York: The Iranian Institute, 1940), p. 240, no. 32; Anthony Welch, *Collection*, vol. 3, Ir. M. 91; idem, *Calligraphy in the Arts of the Muslim World* (Austin and London, 1979), no. 63.

35

## 36 / Marks of Love

By Afzal al-Husayni
Iran, Isfahan; 1646
Page: H. 21.2 cm., W. 30.5 cm.
Miniature: H. 13.1 cm., W. 19.9 cm.

In 1599 the king of Iran, Shah 'Abbas I (r. 1587–1629), dispatched to the courts of Europe a large and impressive embassy whose first secretary was a prominent nobleman, Ulugh Bek. After traveling through Russia, northern and central Europe, and Italy, they arrived in Spain near the end of 1601. To the ambassador's embarrassment, three members of his retinue had abandoned Islam and become Catholics during their stay in Rome; in Spain he was further humiliated by the apostasy of three more leading members of his staff and their conversion to Catholicism. Ulugh Bek was one of the new Christians, and he took the name of Don Juan of Persia. When the ambassador returned to Iran, Don Juan remained in Spain, where he was apparently supported by court funds until his death in a brawl in 1605. His life would be a mere historical anecdote, were it not for the journal he kept from the time he left Iran until his conversion to Catholicism.[1] Without this lively and fascinating document we would be hard pressed to understand what is going on in this painting, but Ulugh Bek–Don Juan provides a vivid elucidation:

> A Persian youth who wishes to pose as a faithful lover must behave in a very extraordinary way; indeed, so strangely that it were impossible for its very extravagance to pass the matter over in silence. The lover who would prove that his love is sincere must painfully burn himself in various parts of his person with a slow match made of linen stuff, that in effect acts exactly like the caustic which, with us in Spain, the surgeons apply for opening issues such as may be needful in the legs and arms. Then the lover displays himself in the sight of his lady, he being a very Lazarus for the number of his sores: whereupon she will send him cloths, napkins and bandages of silk or holland, with which to bind his wounds, and these he wears until they are cured. Later, he who can show most signs of these cauteries is the one most beloved of the fair dames, and he most promptly will come to matrimony.[2]

The young man in this painting must be a prime matrimonial candidate. He is a model of ideal late Safavid beauty: smooth, slightly puffy, round face; softly curving arms, legs, and torso that disavow all implication of muscle; almond-shaped eyes; curving eyebrows that meet over a straight but not too prominent nose; reddish, Cupid's-bow lips; a hint of double chin; and a listless sensuous posture. His lady is slimmer but no less soft and languorous, and both equally are fashion plates in dress. That they are lovers in some degree is made clear by their pose and confirmed by the

**36** / (also in color)

courting birds embroidered on the pillow between them. Wine is a vehicle of transcendence and a metaphor of love, and the golden flask and cup in the lower right are stock motifs in Safavid painting.

The young man placidly endures a variant on Don Juan's trial of love, for his beloved holds the glowing roll of cloth and has already inflicted three marks on his right arm. With his left hand he seems to be asking for more. Other paintings of the Safavid period depict similarly marked young men, and since some of them are dervishes instead of courtly dandies, this proof of love may have been offered to both earthly and divine beloveds.[3]

The inscription at the lower right informs us that the painting was completed in the year 1646 (A.H. 1056) by Afzal al-Husayni, either a student or a close follower of Riza. The large body of work bearing his name is also dated by inscription between 1642 and 1646, indicating a short but productive career. He must have been one of the most favored and prolific traditional painters working in Isfahan, almost surely under the patronage of Shah 'Abbas II (r. 1642–1666), an enthusiastic painting connoisseur of educated and intelligently eclectic taste.[4]

On the reverse are six samples of calligraphy in *naskh* and *nasta'liq* styles: the only one that offers historical information gives the date 1648 (A.H. 1058) and the name 'Abdullah Hamidullah, an otherwise unknown scribe. The page once belonged to a *muraqqa'*, perhaps even the well-known Clive Album, which was compiled during this period. In the Clive Album, in addition to paintings by Riza and his most prominent students, is another painting of the same amorous couple made in the same year by Afzal al-Husayni.[5]

A. W.

1. *Don Juan of Persia,* trans. and ed. with intro. by Guy Le Strange (New York and London, 1926).

2. Ibid., pp. 54–55.

3. See Frederick R. Martin, *The Miniature Paintings and Painters of Persia, India, and Turkey* (London, 1912), vol. 2, pl. 120. For an example from Mughal painting, see Stuart C. Welch and Milo C. Beach, *Gods, Thrones and Peacocks* (New York, 1965), no. 8. For a full description of the same custom among the Khaksar dervishes, see Richard Gramlich, *Schiitische Derwisch-orden,* vol. 3 (Wiesbaden, 1981). Our thanks to Annemarie Schimmel for this reference.

4. For an examination of this ruler's patronage, see Anthony Welch, *Shah 'Abbas and the Arts of Isfahan* (New York, 1973), pp. 84–101.

5. Reproduced in Ivan Stchoukine, *Les Peintures des manuscrits de Shah 'Abbas I à la fin des Safavis* (Paris, 1964), pl. 72; and Basil W. Robinson, *Persian Drawings* (New York, 1965), pl. 63.

PUBLISHED: Anthony Welch, *Collection,* vol. 3, Ir. M. 89.

## 37 / Shah ʿAbbas II and the Mughal Ambassador
Attrib. to Muhammad Zaman
Iran; ca. 1663
Page and miniature: H. 20.3 cm., W. 31.8 cm.

The carpets, the two groups of courtiers and attendants in echelon, and the central figure of the king all direct our attention back toward the palace *eyvan* (arched niche), where a white *thuluth* inscription on a blue background reads: "The Lord of the Court, the Lord of Two Centuries, the Victorious, Shah ʿAbbas II Bahadur Khan. May God make his rule eternal." Over the entrance to a mosque or tomb it might have been a dedicatory identification of donor, but here it serves to explicate the painting, and the ruler's name is divided into its two parts (Shah ʿAbbas II and Bahadur Khan) by the portrait of his head. The shah, in a resplendent turban, his right hand resting on his bejewelled dagger, stares fixedly and coldly at the viewer with a directness rare in Iranian portraiture. The ambassador from the Mughal emperor Awrangzeb (r. 1658–1707) is properly deferential, with his left hand on his *katar* (dagger) and his right extended in dignified obeisance. Musicians in the lower left play *ektar, ʿud,* and tambourine; servants in the upper right carry in trays of food; and eminent onlookers (presumably princes, soldiers, and *vazirs*) flank the principals in the scene. Royal receptions of this sort do figure in earlier Iranian painting, but almost always as illustrations to works of literature.[1]

Certain details of the painting bespeak European influence—the distant trees, the modelling of some of the faces, the all-too-obvious perspective, and the technique of stippling—but the concept and composition come from Mughal India, where the imperial *darbar* (court reception) had been a well-established genre since the reign of Jahangir (1605–1627) and had been one of the most important subjects of painting under Shah Jahan (r. 1628–1658) and during the early reign of his successor Awrangzeb. The *darbar* as a recording of an actual event does not appear in Iran before the seventeenth century. This careful rendering of shah and ambassador recalls Jahangir's charge to Bishndas to record faithfully the appearance of the Iranian ruler Shah ʿAbbas I and suggests that ʿAbbas II may have shared Jahangir's penchant for naturalistic representations of the world around him.[2]

One of the leading Europeanizing masters in seventeenth-century Iran was Muhammad Zaman, who was well acquainted with Indian painting and may have spent time in India.[3] Although this painting is unsigned, its similarities to later work by Muhammad Zaman make an attribution to that master highly plausible. A second depiction of a Mughal ambassador's meeting with the shah was painted by Muhammad Zaman's colleague

37

Shaykh ʿAbbasi (who was also influenced by both European and Indian painting), and is dated to 1663–1664.⁴ It is probable that the two group portraits were painted at approximately the same time.⁵

A. W.

1. See the "Feast of ʿId" from the ca. 1527 manuscript of the *Diwan* of Hafiz (Stuart C. Welch, *A King's Book of Kings* [New York, 1972], fig. 12).

2. See Bishndas's portrait of Shah ʿAbbas I, cat. no. 67. ʿAbbas II's interest in naturalism is evident in the work of Shafiʿ ʿAbbasi (see Anthony Welch, *Shah ʿAbbas and the Arts of Isfahan* [New York, 1973], no. 58).

3. For further discussion of Muhammad Zaman, see ibid., nos. 63, 71, 72, and p. 148.

4. See ibid., no. 62.

5. Another instance of dual representation of a similar scene can be examined in cat. no. 43.

PUBLISHED: Welch, *Shah ʿAbbas and the Arts of Isfahan*, no. 63; idem, *Collection*, vol. 3, Ir. M. 93.

## 38 / Volume One of a *Shahnamah* for Shah ʿAbbas II
Iran, Isfahan; 1654
H. 35.3 cm., W. 24 cm.

Shah ʿAbbas II (r. 1642–1666) was the most effective and active ruler and patron among the later Safavis, and though other patrons were more numerous than in earlier times and undoubtedly were significant in shaping the arts, he played a large role in determining Isfahan's architecture and wider visual culture. As a patron of painting, he was both innovative and eclectic, favoring a number of artists, like Muhammad Zaman, who were influenced by European and Indian art, and encouraging masters like Muʿin who, particularly in his drawings, was exploring new subject matter. But the shah was also a traditionalist and, like his predecessors Tahmasp, Ismaʿil II, and ʿAbbas I, is known to have commissioned a great *Shahnamah*. As its director and chief painter he selected Muʿin Musavvir.

Muʿin's huge talent was already fully developed, and of the fifty-one paintings in this great *Shahnamah*, now divided into two volumes, all but two bear Muʿin's signature.¹ It was an enormous undertaking and a signal honor. Muʿin was only thirty-seven years old when the unidentified scribe finished the book, written in an excellent *nastaʿliq* in four columns of twenty-five lines to the page. The colophon also fails to mention place of production and patron, but since no other city than Isfahan is mentioned in the many inscriptions on Muʿin's works, we can safely assume it was done in the capital. The lavishness of the project and the fact that Muʿin was Riza's most celebrated student make it also likely that the book was produced for the monarch.

Volume 1 of this *Shahnamah* contains a double-page frontispiece and

**38** / folio 12b: Tahmurath defeats the demons

**38** / folio 19b: Faridun strikes Dahhak with his mace

twenty-nine other illustrations. All but two of them are signed by Mu'in. Of the two unsigned pages one is unquestionably his work, which he presumably forgot to sign; the second was apparently added to the volume in the early nineteenth century when the book was rebound in India. The frontispiece is dated to 1656–1657 (A.H. 1067) and appears to have been the last work the painter did on the book; three other illustrations are dated to 1654–1655 (A.H. 1065), and a single painting in the second volume, in the Beatty Library, Dublin, bears the date 1655–1656 (A.H. 1066). Like most manuscript illustrators, Mu'in did not produce his paintings in textual sequence. His signature on all but one of his illustrations is ample indication of Mu'in's high sense of self and of his patron's pride in his artist. The pictures display a consistent style unsurprising in a coherent project accomplished over some three years, and while amply indicating his indebtedness to Riza's training, they also show Mu'in's own flowing line and daring color harmonies within the context of a traditional iconography.

A. W.

1. The second volume is in the Chester Beatty Library, Dublin (see A. J. Arberry, B. W. Robinson, E. Blochet, and J. V. S. Wilkinson, *The Chester Beatty Library, a Catalogue of the Persian Manuscripts and Miniatures* [Dublin, 1962], vol. 3, Ms. 270).

PUBLISHED: Anthony Welch, *Shah 'Abbas and the Arts of Isfahan* (New York, 1973), no. 57; idem, *Collection*, vol. 4, Ms. 22.

## 39 / An Isfahan Dandy

By Mu'in Musavvir
Iran, Isfahan; ca. 1660
Page: H. 37 cm., W. 24.2 cm.
Miniature: H. 13.2 cm., W. 4.9 cm.

This self-complacent young man poses in what must have been the latest and highest fashion. A bright yellow flower and a black feather stick jauntily in his pink turban; his violet overcoat, lined with flowered silk, hangs open over his brown undergarment and yellow trousers. Sleek, affluent, empty-headed, and distinctly unheroic, he and his like were the beau ideals of Safavid society and the subjects of many hundreds of Safavid pictures.

No one recorded these feckless youths (the living embodiments of the ideal beloved in Iranian poetry) better than two masters, Riza[1] and his star pupil Mu'in, who signed this portrait in his unmistakable hand. Trained by Riza in the last years of that artist's life, Mu'in Musavvir had an extraordinarily long career; dated works bearing his name span the years from 1635 to 1707. He was also enormously productive, in fact the most prolific (as well as one of the most gifted) of all Iranian painters, and his single-

39

page drawings and paintings, as well as his many manuscript illustrations,[2] provide us with an abundance of material for understanding the career and personality of one of the most remarkable figures in Iranian art history. Faithful to his training, he preserved his Safavid heritage and refrained from any significant Europeanizing, despite the vogue for European art at the royal court. He was in the employ of four successive monarchs but seems to have been free to work for others as well, since many patrons are cited in the often lengthy inscriptions he provided on his pictures: such is the wealth and diversity of his epigraphic information that one suspects him either of a secret longing to write history or of a profound sympathy with the needs of future historians. His prominent signature on so many paintings testifies not to an overpowering ego but to a simple desire to keep facts straight. His versatility is exceptional, and his range of subject matter extends from traditional epics like the *Shahnamah* to contemporary dandies like this one and to topical documentary drawings of daily life. It is through his eyes that we may see seventeenth-century Isfahan.[3]

A. W.

1. For a version of the same theme by Riza, see cat. no. 34.
2. For Mu'in's great *Shahnamah* illustrations, see cat. no. 38.
3. Additional works and further information on Mu'in can be found in Anthony Welch, *Shah 'Abbas and the Arts of Isfahan* (New York, 1973), nos. 56, 57, 76, 77, 78, 79, 85, and pp. 147–48.

PUBLISHED: Anthony Welch, *Collection*, vol. 1, Ir. M. 44.

## 40 / European Youth with an Iranian Pot
by Mu'in Musavvir
Iran, Isfahan; August–September 1673
Miniature: H. 19.3 cm., W. 9.2 cm.

Mu'in Musavvir appreciated strong colors, and this fascinating portrait uses a predominantly warm palette—orange socks, pink pantaloons, a burgundy coat, and a brown hat. They are set off by the youth's green shirt and the large white pot, decorated with a pale blue crane, that he carries in both hands. Despite his clothing, which conforms to Western European fashion of the 1630s, the young man's slightly wistful face and his curving posture are seventeenth-century Iranian; it is unlikely that this is a portrait of a specific European visitor.

Mu'in often paid fealty to his revered teacher, Riza-yi 'Abbasi, by making copies or adaptations of his master's works.[1] This picture is one of them, but the evidence is a bit indirect. In March–April 1635, Mu'in completed initial work on a portrait of Riza; the older painter died the following

40 /

month. The famous portrait[2] shows Riza seated at work on a picture of a European youth holding a large ceramic pot; since Riza's painting was still in progress, the pot was still undecorated and lacked a top. In other respects the picture in Riza's hands is identical with this 1673 painting by Mu'in.

Riza still had a month to live at the time Mu'in did his initial work on the portrait in 1635, and he presumably finished the picture of the European youth. Mu'in did not complete his portrait of Riza. Perhaps too affected by grief at his master's death, he did not turn to it again until his own son requested him to, and as he carefully notes, he finally finished the portrait of Riza on 24 December 1673, a few months after he had painted his own version of Riza's European youth with an Iranian pot. Mu'in either owned Riza's original or had it in his possession long enough to make his version of it. That original is apparently no longer extant but is doubly recorded for us through Mu'in's portrait of Riza at work and through his version of Riza's picture.

A. W.

1. See cat. no. 41.
2. Now in the Princeton University Library and reproduced in Ernst Grube, *Muslim Miniature Painting* (Venice, 1962), no. 118; and Anthony Welch, *Shah 'Abbas and the Arts of Isfahan* (New York, 1973), no. 76.

## 41 / The Royal Physician, Hakim Shafa'i

By Mu'in Musavvir
Iran, Isfahan; 21 April 1674
Page: H. 30.5 cm., W. 21.1 cm.
Miniature: H. 18.5 cm., W. 9.8 cm.

Physicians occupied an honored place in Safavid society, and medical doctors at the royal court sometimes held important offices of state as well. High position held its risks, of course. Not only could intrigues or unsuccessful policies undermine the physician-as-politician, but the physician's medical standing depended upon the health of the shah, and most of the Safavids were notorious for health-impairing addictions and overindulgences in wine or drugs. The vicissitudes of one of the physicians to Shah 'Abbas I (r. 1587–1629) were probably typical for many of his colleagues. Hakim Rukna was descended from a long line of physicians who had served at court, and he added talents as a poet and calligrapher to his medical skills. Some time during the 1590s 'Abbas sickened, and though the king recovered, he did not credit Hakim Rukna with the cure but instead fired him and ordered him to pay back all his previous salary. After losing everything he owned, the doctor left the capital city with his family,

41 /

practiced medicine elsewhere, failed to regain the royal favor, and like so many other skilled Iranians in the Safavid period, left Iran for India. There his fortunes recovered; as physician to the Mughal emperor Jahangir he soon became a rich man.[1]

The inscription at the top of this page identifies it as a "portrait of the Plato of the Age, Hakim Shafa'i."[2] This *hakim* (doctor), a more fortunate contemporary of the misused Hakim Rukna, also served as physician-in-attendance to Shah 'Abbas I, but he was not accused of malpractice, outlived his patient, and continued as royal doctor under Shah Safi I (r. 1629–1642). A second inscription, under the physician's legs, dates the painting to the fifteenth day of the holy month of Muharram in the year 1085 (21 April 1674) and states that it was done by Mu'in Musavvir. The words in the lower left add that this portrait was based on an earlier picture painted by Riza-yi 'Abbasi in 1634–1635 (A.H. 1044), the last year of Riza's life. These last two inscriptions, in Mu'in's hand, typify his penchant for historical data.

Riza's earlier portrait has fortunately been preserved.[3] Although the sitter wears different-colored clothing, he adopts the same pose and is unquestionably the same individual. An inscription on the painting reads, "Portrait of Hakim Shafa'i by the humble Riza Musavvir." Forty years later, either on his own initiative or on commission, Mu'in produced his version of the portrait; the identifying inscription at the top of the page, however, was supplied by someone else.[4]

The high status of successful royal doctors accounts for the very formal nature of this fine portrait. Mu'in's *hakim* wears clothing subdued in tone: a light brown overgarment, a lavender undergarment, and light blue leggings. His purple, yellow, and white sash is laced with gold, as is his multicolored (blue, white, and red) turban. The landscape setting accentuates the sitter, for it is sparse, with faint gold clouds, leaves, and stones, and the only other color is in the objects in front of Shafa'i that signify his learned profession: two books (one surely must be the works of Avicenna, the chief source of medical information in Safavid Iran), scissors, a white inkpot, and a pen-box. The doctor appears about fifty years old, and his wrinkled brow, raised left eyebrow, and barely suppressed grin give him a slightly bemused appearance.

A. W.

1. See Qadi Ahmad, *Calligraphers and Painters,* trans. Vladimir Minorsky (Washington, D.C., 1959), p. 169; and Anthony Welch, *Artists for the Shah* (New Haven and London, 1976), p. 11.

2. "Plato of the Age" was an honorific frequently awarded to physicians.

3. British Museum, 1920–9–17–0298(2).

4. Bibliothèque Nationale, Paris, Sup. pers. 1572, fol. 3, is a third portrait of Hakim Shafa'i, painted somewhat later than Mu'in's.

PUBLISHED: Thomas W. Arnold, "Some Unpublished Persian Paintings of the Safavid Period," *Journal of Indian Art and Letters,* no. 135 (July 1916), pl. 1; Ernst Kühnel, "Der Maler, Mu'in," *Pantheon* 29 (1942):113; Ivan Stchoukine, *Les Peintures des manuscrits de Shah 'Abbas I à la fin des Safavis* (Paris, 1964), pp. 67–68; Anthony Welch, *Collection,* vol. 3, Ir. M. 95.

## 42 / Two Shepherds in a Bucolic Landscape
By 'Ali Quli Jabbahdar
Iran; ca. 1675
Page and miniature: H. 12.1 cm., W. 16.9 cm.

Contoured ground of this sort is not part of the Iranian landscape tradition, and the trees seem more suited to European than to Iranian art. Though the dreamy youth seated at the right is conventional in seventeenth-century painting in Iran, his bare legs are not, and the awkwardly posed flutist is foreign in clothes and occupation. Despite its two bulbous domes, the cluster of presumably wooden brown buildings in the background is, like the blue-streaked sky, closer to Europe than Iran. European prints were traded and admired in Iran as well as India in the sixteenth and seventeenth centuries, but this small painting seems to be an original work and not a copy.[1]

An inscription at the left gives the name of the painter, 'Ali Quli Jabbahdar. He came to Iran from an unspecified European country and seems to have worked primarily for provincial nobles rather than for the royal house.[2] He was obviously not a European painter of the first rank, but his foreign origin and techniques gained him prominence outside his own cultural tradition.[3]

A. W.

1. A Mughal copy of this painting is in the Musée Guimet, Paris. Either the picture was at one time in India, or both paintings are based upon a common print.
2. A celebrated album now in Leningrad contains several pages of his work. An inscription on one miniature states that it was completed in 1674 in Qazvin, at that time an important provincial city but not the capital; two other miniatures bear inscriptions in Georgian, and it is reasonable to conclude that 'Ali Quli was in the service of one of the Georgian nobles who were prominent supporters of the Safavid royal house.
3. For further information on 'Ali Quli Jabbahdar, see Anthony Welch, *Shah 'Abbas and the Arts of Isfahan* (New York, 1973), pp. 148–49.

PUBLISHED: Anthony Welch, *Collection,* vol. 1, Ir. M. 42; A. Welch, *Shah 'Abbas and the Arts of Isfahan,* no. 73.

42 /

Isfandiyar kills the *simurgh*. Cat. no. 29(B)

Ibrahim Mirza's garden party. Cat. no. 30, folio 86b

Bazindah and the sudden storm. Cat. no. 32, folio 22a

*Page Boy with Bottle and Cup.* Cat. no. 34

*Marks of Love.* Cat. no. 36

Fath ʿAli Shah. Cat. no. 44, folio 3b

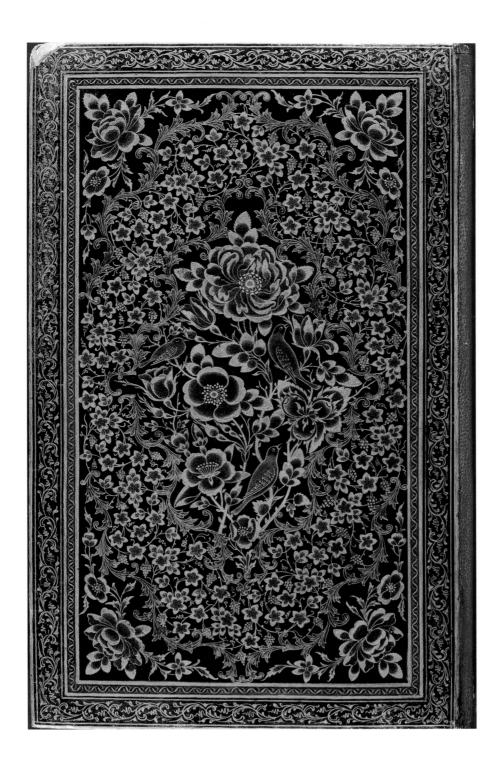

Binding for a manuscript of Muhammad Baqir's *Zad al-Ma'ad*. Cat. no. 46

*A Family of Cheetahs.* Cat. no. 50

*Flight of a* Simurgh. Cat. no. 57

A prince and a hermit. Cat. no. 59(A)

*A Noble Hunt.* Cat. no. 65

*Jahangir at the* Jharoka *Window.* Cat. no. 69

*Tulips and an Iris.* Cat. no. 72

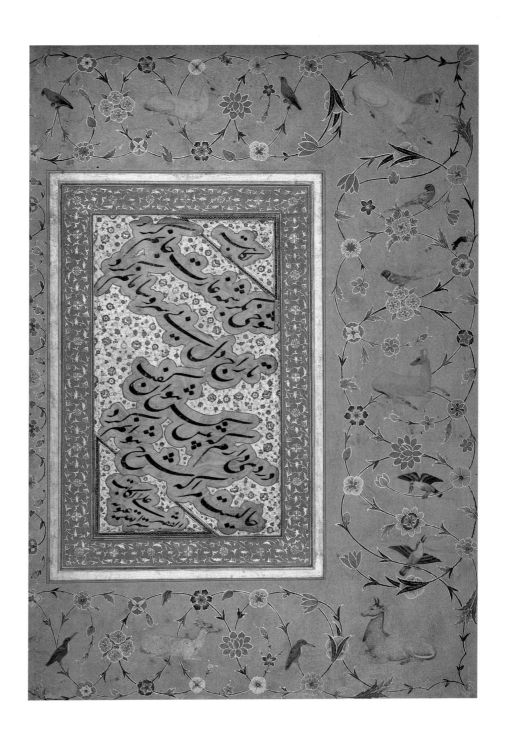

*A Love Poem.* Cat. no. 73

*A Floral Fantasy.* Cat. no. 75

*Colonel Polier's* Nautch. Cat. no. 79

## 43 / Portraits of a Notable Russian
Iran, Isfahan; 1716–1717
(A) By ʿAli Quli Jabbahdar
   Page: H. 31 cm., W. 20.8 cm.
   Miniature: H. 16.8 cm., W. 12.1 cm.
(B) By Muhammad Zaman
   Page: H. 31 cm., W. 18.9 cm.
   Miniature: H. 16.5 cm., W. 8.6 cm.

Although idealized images of beautiful youths abound in Safavid art, realistic portraiture was also an important genre, particularly in the seventeenth century. Not only were Iranians of various social classes and professions represented but pictures of foreigners were commissioned, sometimes on royal command. In the Topkapi Palace Museum in Istanbul is an album containing facing-page portraits of two Russian dignitaries, perhaps merchants or diplomats, both pages bearing the seal of Shah ʿAbbas I.[1] If that early seventeenth-century *muraqqaʿ* was still in Safavid royal possession a hundred years later, it may have served as inspiration for the two portraits shown here, which may also have faced each other in an album made for the last ruling Safavid shah, Sultan Husayn (r. 1694–1722). Both are inscribed and dated. Number 43(A) is simply annotated in the upper left with the name of the painter, ʿAli Quli, and the date A.H. 1129 (1716–1717). Number 43(B) bears more extensive notes: it was done in the same year by Muhammad Zaman on the orders of the shah. In neither portrait is the sitter identified.

Three different Russian embassies were sent by Peter the Great to the court of Shah Sultan Husayn at Isfahan in 1697, 1708, and 1717, and presumably there were Russians among the many merchants who did business in Isfahan during that period. Whoever he was, this particular Russian aroused special interest in the otherwise lackadaisical monarch, for he evidently ordered his two most experienced Europeanizing masters to portray him.[2]

A. W.

1. Topkapi Palace Museum, H. 2155, fols. 19b and 20a. Though neither is signed, one can be attributed to Riza and the other, tentatively, to Sadiqi Bek.
2. For ʿAli Quli, see cat. no. 42; for Muhammad Zaman, see cat. no. 37. It is possible that these portraits were not made from life but were instead based upon an earlier painting that the shah admired and wished to have reproduced in his album. A. A. Ivanov, T. B. Grek, and O. Akimushkin, *Album indiskikh i persidskikh miniatur XVI–XVIII v.* [Album of Indian and Persian Miniatures, Sixteenth–Eighteenth Centuries] (Moscow, 1962), publish an invaluable discussion of Muhammad Zaman and ʿAli Quli, as well as a number of paintings by them.

PUBLISHED: Anthony Welch, *Shah ʿAbbas and the Arts of Isfahan* (New York, 1973), no. 86; idem, *Collection*, vol. 3, Ir. M. 97 and Ir. M. 98.

**43A** / Portrait of a notable Russian

**43B** / Portrait of a notable Russian

## 44 / Album of Portraits and Calligraphies

Iran, Tehran; ca. 1819
H. 29.3 cm., W. 19.7 cm.

Most albums are bound as books, but the sixteen pages of this early nineteenth-century Qajar *muraqqaʿ* are hinged together so they fold out, presenting a series of portraits and calligraphies of high quality. The portraits have a single theme—Iranian kingship, and twelve historical or legendary rulers are represented. This demonstration of royal succession was presumably intended to bolster the Qajar dynasty's sense of legitimacy: Fath ʿAli Shah, whose portrait is the album's first, was only the second king of this line. Some of the monarchs are identified by inscription, and our identification of the remaining shahs is based upon their resemblance to other portraits.[1] The portraits are not organized chronologically:

fol. 3b:   Fath ʿAli Shah (r. 1797–1834). The portrait (illustrated) bears his name and is dated to 1819 (A.H. 1234); the throne is inscribed with a panegyric verse.

fol. 4a:   Aqa Muhammad Shah (r. 1779–1797), identified by name.

fol. 5b:   Probably Shah ʿAbbas I (r. 1587–1629).

fol. 6a:   Probably Shah ʿAbbas II (r. 1642–1666).

fol. 7b:   Probably Jamshid, one of the great rulers and culture heroes in Firdausi's *Shahnamah.*

fol. 14a:  Kay Kaʾus, another monarch from the *Shahnamah,* identified by name.

fol. 9b:   Probably Ismaʿil I (r. 1501–1524), founder of the Safavid dynasty.

fol. 10a:  Nadir Shah (r. 1736–1747). There is no inscription, but the portrait is very similar to other, contemporary portraits.

fol. 11b:  Genghis Khan (?1167–1227), identified by name.

fol. 12a:  A Central Asian ruler, almost certainly Timur (?1336–1405).

fol. 13b:  Karim Khan Zand (1750–1797).

fol. 14a:  Kay Kaʾus, another monarch from the *Shahnamah,* identified by name.

Each of the pre-Qajar rulers is associated with a period of particular Iranian strength and prestige, and it seems reasonable to assume that Fath ʿAli Shah was being favorably compared with them.

The album's other pages are devoted to calligraphy and demonstrate the various styles of script that were in use in early Qajar Iran: they include fine examples of *shikastah, thuluth, naskh,* and *nastaʿliq.* Five of the twenty calligraphies are signed or dated or both:

fol. 1b:   a page of *naskh,* dated to 1813 (A.H. 1228).

fol. 2a:   a page of *naskh,* dated to 1813 (A.H. 1228) and signed by Abu'l-Qasim Shirazi.[2]

44 / folio 3b: Fath ʿAli Shah (also in color)

fol. 12b:      a page of *shikastah*, done in Isfahan in 1715 (A.H. 1127) and signed by Muhammad Hashim.3

fol. 13a:      a page of four scripts—*shikastah, thuluth, naskh,* and *nasta'liq*—dated to 1813 (A.H. 1228).

fol. 15a:      a page of *shikastah*, dated to 1810 (A.H. 1225) and signed by Muhammad Ja'far.4

Fath 'Ali Shah was an accomplished calligrapher, though his own work is not included here.5 And although most albums contained samples of the writing of celebrated past masters like Mir 'Ali or Mir 'Imad, this *muraqqa'* is restricted to the art of contemporary or recent masters of the eighteenth or early nineteenth century.

In one sense the album is a careful pictorial panegyric of kingship; in another it is an exercise in "modernism" that may have been dictated by Fath 'Ali Shah's personal taste. Almost certainly, the *muraqqa'* was commissioned by him or was offered to him by a close associate or hopeful courtier.

A. W.

1. Basil W. Robinson has pointed out to me in a letter that Fath 'Ali Shah commissioned his court painter Mihr 'Ali to paint a number of historical portraits for the walls of the Imarat-i Naw palace in Isfahan, and it is possible that the royal portraits in this album were based upon them.

2. See M. Bayani, *Khushnevisan* [Calligraphers] (Tehran, 1966), pp. 32–33.

3. Ibid., pp. 859–60.

4. Ibid., pp. 672–73.

5. For an example of his calligraphy, see Anthony Welch, *Collection,* vol. 3, Cal. 12; and idem, *Calligraphy in the Arts of the Muslim World* (Austin and London, 1979), no. 67.

PUBLISHED: Anthony Welch, *Collection,* vol. 4, Ms. 23.

## 45 / Elephant Attacked by Wolves

Iran; ca. 1850
Page: H. 40.5 cm., W. 26.4 cm.
Miniature: H. 27.5 cm., W. 19 cm.

Under an illuminated arch (added later to the page), a domesticated elephant fights off attack by ten wolves, many of whom it has already disabled. Though an Indian subject, this ink drawing was produced in Qajar Iran. Neither patron nor artist is identified. Arabic and Persian verses above and below the drawing are also later additions: they are love poems, unrelated to the subject of the picture, that were appended when the drawing was attached to its present mount, either for inclusion in an album or for sale by a dealer.

A. W.

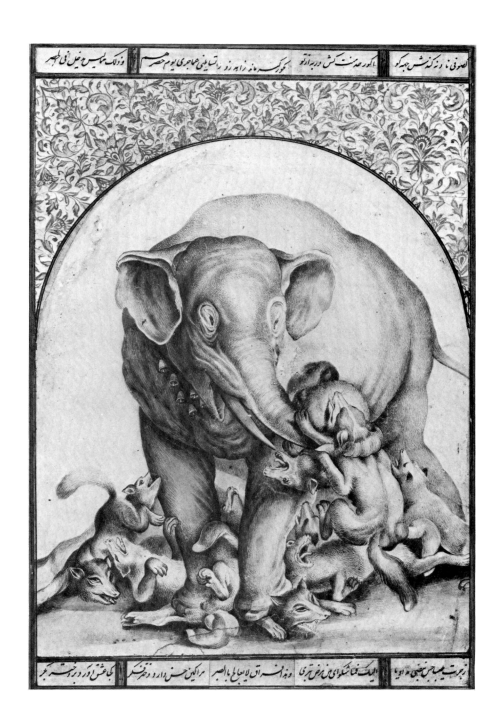

ایرت بیماجس نبی واوا  الیک فتا شکوای ازبرض تربا  وهذا اسراق لایجا لح بالصبر  اراکین حسن زار و دنیر فسر  یک عش اور و دربسته بج

45

135

**46** / Binding (also in color)

**46** / A Manuscript of Muhammad Baqir's *Zad al-Ma'ad*
Iran, Tehran; 1895–1896
H. 22.3 cm., W. 14 cm.

Although widespread before the sixteenth century, Twelver Shi'ism[1] became Iran's official state religion only with the advent of the Safavid dynasty in 1501, and the faith's expansion throughout the country was an essential part of the Safavid consolidation of power. Theologically, this early period was less important than the late seventeenth century, when the Safavid state itself was in decline but its religious thinkers were extremely active. Muhammad Baqir (1627–1699), son of a leading theologian, held the high offices of Shaykh al-Islam under Shah Sulayman (r. 1666–1694) and Mulla Bashi under Shah Sultan Husayn (r. 1694–1722). Until his death he was one of the dominant figures in government and encouraged persecution of religious minorities like the Sunni Muslims, Jews, Christians, and Zoroastrians. His religious politics contributed materially to the collapse of the Safavid state in 1722.

Of longer lasting significance were his theological works, which are still influential in present-day Iran. The twenty-five-volume *Bahr al-Anwar* (*Ocean of Lights*) is an Arabic compilation of Shi'a *Hadith* (traditional religious sayings of the Prophet) and was perhaps his most important contribution. The *Zad al-Ma'ad* (Provisions for the Resurrection) is a one-volume abridgment of it, made expressly for those too busy to consult the massive original treatise. It comprises Arabic prayers for each day of the year with titles and explanatory introductions to each prayer written in Persian.

This particularly fine manuscript of the *Zad al-Ma'ad* has twelve lines of text on most of its 120 pages. It is written in a clear *naskh* style by a fine, though unidentified, scribe. The dark brown lacquer binding is illuminated with gold birds and flowers on the exterior (illustrated) and a single gold iris on the interior, where there is also an inscription stating that the illumination was the work of the head gilder, Mahmud Shirazi, on the order of his "glorious and august majesty," in the year 1895–1896 (A.H. 1313). Shah Nasr al-Din Qajar was assassinated in that year, and the inscription could refer either to him or to his son and successor, Muzaffar al-Din.

A. W.

1. Twelver Shi'ism accepts the succession of twelve imams after the death of the Prophet Muhammad; Isma'ilis accept seven imams.

PUBLISHED: Anthony Welch, *Collection*, vol. 4, Ms. 25.

# *India*

In 711, Arab Muslim armies conquered Sind (present-day southern Pakistan), and Muslim merchants settled in various commercial centers in western and southern India. By the beginning of the tenth century there was an important Isma'ili community in Multan (modern central Pakistan). Muslim armies from Afghanistan raided northern India in the tenth and eleventh centuries, but it is with the establishment of the Delhi sultanate in 1191 that Islam arrived in India to stay. From its base in Delhi the sultanate expanded steadily in northern and central India, using a combination of military operations and energetic proselytizing. In its early decades the sultanate depended heavily upon imported talent for its administration and its culture, but by the second half of the thirteenth century a distinctive Indian Islamic culture is discernible. Great poets like Amir Khusraw Dehlevi were writing in Persian; in the fourteenth century architects and builders under the aegis of the Tughluq dynasty (1320–1398) were creating the sultanate's most impressive architectural style, while calligraphers were developing definably Indo-Muslim styles of writing.

But it was under the Mughals (1526–1540; 1555–1858) that Islamic culture in India acquired the stamp of distinctive personalities. Contemporary histories, biographies, and travelers' accounts allow us to see in detail the Mughals' India, while the memoirs, autobiographies, and personal letters left by nearly every Mughal ruler give us intimate glimpses of their characters, aspirations, and aesthetics. India's fabled wealth attracted the first Mughal, Babur, to leave his Timurid patrimony in Central Asia and conquer Delhi in 1526, and his vivid *Memoirs*, based on notes and composed during his four short years of rule from 1526 to 1530, established a model of royal memoir for his successors. His son Humayun's rule was checkered by setbacks and misfortunes, and he was briefly in exile in Shah Tahmasp's Iran, where he met and subsequently enticed to India Safavid masters who were instrumental in creating Mughal painting.

It was under Humayun's astonishing son Akbar (r. 1556–1605) that the Mughal state and Mughal art took definitive form. Nearly annual military campaigns expanded the empire to include two-thirds of India. His administrative genius created an efficient centralized bureaucratic government that sustained his successors for more than a hundred years. A passionate builder, he transformed the architectural face of India with a profusion of brilliantly designed cities, forts, caravansaries, mosques, and palaces, and though himself illiterate, he was a dynamic patron of literature and the arts of the precious book. His patronage of histories, literary classics, and Persian translations of Hindu sacred texts reflected his roots in Islamic tradition, and his taste in art was similarly energetic and eclectic. Throughout his long reign he supported a huge atelier of painters, calligraphers, and other manuscript artisans and oversaw the emergence of a Mughal synthesis of Iranian, indigenous Indian, and European styles in painting. The Mughals were patrons in the Timurid tradition, and from its inception Mughal painting was dynasty-oriented and inclined to realism and truthful observation of the natural world.

Akbar's questing intellect even led him for some time to separate himself apparently from strict Muslim orthodoxy by creating at his court a small elite group intended to adhere to the noblest principles of all the religions he admired. This course his son and successor Jahangir (r. 1605–1627) considered deviant. More orthodox and less ambitious, Jahangir was a consolidator, who relegated much of his authority to subordinates. Less interested in architecture, he was a brilliant patron of the portable arts, particularly painting and calligraphy. But he reduced the size of the imperial atelier and emphasized quality over quantity and single-page paintings over lengthy manuscripts. Akbar had been fascinated with the depiction of action; Jahangir focused more on forms and their inner essence, and the production of his atelier tended to portraits—highly personal studies of people, animals, or plants that reflect the emperor's refined taste and his eager fascination with the forms of life around him.

Under Shah Jahan (r. 1627–1657) the inner warmth and vitality of earlier Mughal painting seems more restrained, replaced by crystalline formality. Like the immaculate beauty of the Taj Mahal with its jeweled inlays, pictorial arts take on a lapidary aspect, immobile, set, and the people depicted seem to move with increasingly courtly dignity. The Mughal empire was at its richest, and the emperor devoted himself to the rituals of office with painstaking assiduity.

Bitter rivalries for power had seen both Jahangir and Shah Jahan rebel against their fathers, and brutal civil wars at the end of Shah Jahan's reign ended with the victory of Awrangzeb (r. 1657–1707). Although a discerning and enthusiastic patron of art during the early years of his reign, Awrangzeb turned increasingly to statecraft and piety. He briefly brought almost the entire subcontinent under Mughal rule but broke his empire in so doing. First in the Deccan and then in northern India, Muslim states separated from central rule, until the Mughal empire was a truncated and emaciated remnant of its seventeenth-century glory. European powers had coveted India's wealth for generations, and after the collapse of Mughal power in the eighteenth century the Muslim and Hindu states of India were methodically brought under British domination. Even in this period of decline and foreign rule India's pictorial tradition remained vital, preserving past achievement and absorbing and transforming the new.

A. W.

## 47 / A Manuscript of the Qur'an
India, Gwalior Fort; 1399
H. 24 cm., W. 17 cm.

Medieval India's longest-lived Muslim dynasty was that of the Tughluqs, who controlled the north and dominated much of central India from 1320 to 1388, when the last effective sultan, Firuz Shah, died. His successors warred among themselves for a decade, and the internecine feuding so weakened the once powerful sultanate that formerly tributary provinces, both Muslim and Hindu, became autonomous, while the kingdom's celebrated wealth made it a tempting target for the Central Asian conqueror Timur. In 1398–1399, at a time when the capital of Delhi itself was split between two rival claimants to the throne, Timur invaded and drove the Tughluqs from their city, which he toured and much admired before sacking it with his usual thoroughness.

This Qur'an, one of the most important medieval Muslim manuscripts, was probably begun in Delhi before Timur's visit. It may have been commissioned by one of the sultanate's two contending kings, Mahmud or Nusrat. It was not finished there, for in the Persian colophon the scribe, Mahmud Sha'ban, writes that he finished this copy of the scripture on 7 Dhu'l-qa'da 801 (21 July 1399)[1] in Gwalior Fort, a massive military complex south of Agra. He probably fled again soon afterward, for the fort, never attacked by Timur, was seized by Hindu Rajputs.

This Qur'an has 550 pages and is written in the Bihari style, a regional variant of eastern *naskh* that was restricted to India. *Surah* headings are written in a large Kufic. An interlinear translation into Persian, written in a smaller and more cursive style of script, indicates that its patron was not wholly at ease with Arabic. All three script styles are probably the work of the same calligrapher. Thirty-four double pages are also lavishly illuminated with bold, dense, and intensely colorful floral and vegetal arrangements—in blue, white, yellow, gold, black, red, and brown—that are far more luxuriant than the illumination in contemporary Qur'ans from Muslim lands to the west. Altogether, the manuscript is one of the most beautiful and significant documents for the history of Sultanate India.

A. W.

47 / folio 2a: frontispiece

47 / folio 1b: frontispiece

1. This Qur'an was first identified and published by Simon Digby, to whose knowledge I am extremely indebted. Annemarie Schimmel has noted that the form for *8* is most unusual and can only be reconstituted.

PUBLISHED: *The Arts of Islam* (exhib. cat.; London: Hayward Gallery, 1976), no. 635; Anthony Welch, *Calligraphy in the Arts of the Muslim World* (Austin and London, 1979), no. 75.

## 48 / The Night of Power

India; ca. 1350–1450
From a manuscript of the *Khamsah* of Amir Khusraw Dehlevi
Page: H. 34.3 cm., W. 25.3 cm.
Miniature: H. 8 cm., W. 20.1 cm.

This page originally belonged to a manuscript of the *Khamsah* (Quintet) of Amir Khusraw Dehlevi, one of the most celebrated Indian poets writing in Persian. His long life (1253–1325) spanned the period in which Islam established itself as the governing authority in northern India, and he himself belonged to the Turkish military aristocracy that provided the ruling elite. Amir Khusraw served under a number of Turkish Muslim nobles in northwestern and northern India until 1290, when he entered the Delhi sultan's service, and he enjoyed the patronage of kings of the Khalji and Tughluq dynasties. A prominent disciple of the great Chishti Sufi Nizam al-Din Awliya, the poet was buried next to the saint in the Nizamuddin *dargah* (Sufi center) in Delhi. Among his many works the *Khamsah*, written between 1298–1299 and 1301–1302, is probably best known.

The miniature illustrates the tale of a saint who attempted (and failed) to stay awake until the Night of Power (*layla al-qadar*), the twenty-seventh day of Ramadan. The central image of *surah* 97 of the Qur'an, the Night of Power refers to the evening on which Muhammad was first called to his mission, when the first verses of the Qur'an were revealed.

If this copy of the *Khamsah* had a colophon, it was lost when the manuscript was broken up, and the dating of this key Sultanate work remains in dispute, with evidence and arguments ranging from mid-fourteenth- to mid-fifteenth-century northern India and from royal to nonroyal patrons.[1]

A. W.

1. Richard Ettinghausen, *Paintings of the Sultans and Emperors of India* (Delhi, 1961), noted the *Khamsah's* stylistic affinities with both Mamluk Egyptian and southern Iranian painting of the second half of the fourteenth century, but on the basis of the manuscript's calligraphic style, admittedly rather unimpressive, dated it to the second half of the fifteenth century. A. S. Melikian Chirvani, "L'école de Shiraz et les origines de la miniature moghole," in *Paintings from Islamic Lands*, ed. Ralph Pinder-Wilson (Oxford, 1969), has suggested an earlier date for both text and illustrations. A close stylistic comparison in painting is found in a late fifteenth-century *Shahnamah* produced in northern India (see Moti Chandra, *Studies in Early Indian Painting* [Bombay, 1970], cpl. X). Karl Khandalavala and Moti Chandra, *New Documents of*

*Indian Painting—A Reappraisal* (Bombay, 1969), date the *Khamsah* to the second quarter of the fifteenth century and suggest that it was not done for a royal patron. Most recently Milo C. Beach, *The Imperial Image: Paintings for the Mughal Court* (Washington, D.C., 1981), pp. 42–46, has leaned toward a dating in the second half of the fourteenth century. This view seems the most plausible, and it would suggest that the patron may have been the Sultan Firuz Shah (r. 1351–1388), whose uncle, Sultan Ghiyath al-Din (r. 1320–1325), had established the Tughluq dynasty in Delhi. Ghiyath al-Din was the last notable patron of Amir Khusraw Dehlevi, who wrote a *Tughluqnamah* in his praise.

**49** / Portrait of Shah Abu'l-Ma'ali
By Dust Muhammad
India; ca. 1556–1560
Page: H. 33.7 cm., W. 24.6 cm.
Miniature: H. 17.5 cm., W. 14.5 cm.

A young man sits writing, his right hand holding a tiny red pen and his left hand supporting the paper propped on his right knee. Like a turtle poking out of his shell, his slender neck and round head emerge from his clothes (a pale yellow coat open over a pale blue garment), topped by a turban of a style fashionable during the reign of Akbar's father, Humayun. There is no background. The back's too perfect (and too shell-like) curve and the oddly projecting shoulder look unnatural, and the smooth, intent face seems tight and troubled. Neither paper nor person are quite balanced.

On the sheet is written: "God is Great. Jannat Ashiani.[1] This portrait is the likeness of Shah Abu'l-Ma'ali of Kashgar, whom his Majesty keeps close to him in royal service. The work of Master Dust Musavvir." The words *Jannat Ashiani* refer to someone already dead, and were used as a posthumous title for Humayun. The picture was therefore made after Humayun's death in 1556 and was probably commissioned by the sitter, who enjoyed far less favor under Akbar.[2]

Shah Abu'l-Ma'ali had been one of Humayun's closest friends: the second Mughal ruler had even adopted him as his son. But to Akbar and to almost everyone associated with him Abu'l-Ma'ali was overbearing, untrustworthy, and disloyal, "a repository of strife and sedition" and a "brainless and ill-fated youth" whose "brain had been ruined by the worship of his own beauty."[3] He was also a murderer. Abu'l-Fazl wrote of him with dislike and contempt:

Shah Abu'l-Ma'ali traced his descent from the sayyids of Termiz. His personal beauty made the good and right-thinking look for goodness of nature, and his forwardness was tolerated on account of his courage. Conse-

**49**

quently he became a favorite of His Majesty Jahanbani [Humayun]. Some of his insolencies and extravagancies will be related in their proper place.[4]

Since the final years of his turbulent life were spent in sedition and rebellion, this portrait must have been completed in the first three or four years of Akbar's reign, when Shah Abu'l-Ma'ali still enjoyed royal favor.

The painter, Master Dust Musavvir, was also known as Dust-i Divana and Dust Muhammad.[5] He grew up in Herat in the late fifteenth and early sixteenth centuries, studied with the celebrated painter Bihzad, and probably accompanied him to the Safavid court in Tabriz in 1522. An accomplished calligrapher as well as painter, he remained with Shah Tahmasp until mid-century, when he took up Humayun's earlier invitation and left for Mughal territory. He worked first for Humayun's brother Kamran in Kabul and, after Kamran's death in 1550, for Humayun. The use here of the title *Jannat Ashiani* suggests that he also served under Akbar, though since Abu'l-Fazl does not see fit to mention him among the Iranian painters at court, it could not have been for long. His influence on Mughal painting is indiscernible, and this portrait must number among his very last Indian pictures.

The portrait is mounted on an eighteenth-century album leaf. On the reverse are four lines of poetry, penned in *nasta'liq* style by Muhammad Riza.[6]

> You have become afflicted by that coquette.
> You have become a friend of sorrows and pains.
> You have the bowl of your eye in your hand,
> Saying: "I have become a beggar from seeing you."

A. W.

1. Meaning "Nested in Paradise."
2. A portrait drawn above an adulatory couplet and attributed to Mir Sayyid 'Ali has been recognized as a somewhat earlier likeness of Shah Abu'l-Ma'ali (see Stuart C. Welch, *Indian Drawings and Painted Sketches* [New York, 1976], no. 3).
3. Abu'l-Fazl, *The Akbarnama*, trans. H. Blochmann (Calcutta, 1907), 2:153, 309, 27.
4. Ibid., 1:580.
5. For a full account of this extraordinary artist, calligrapher, and man of letters, see Martin B. Dickson and Stuart C. Welch, *The Houghton Shahnameh* (Cambridge, Mass., 1981), especially pp. 118–28. This volume includes discussion of Shah Abu'l-Ma'ali, his career, crimes, and portraits.
6. The name is not uncommon among calligraphers, but the scribe here may be the same master who designed some of the inscriptions in the Royal Mosque of Isfahan and in the Shrine of Imam Riza in Mashhad (see Anthony Welch, *Shah 'Abbas and the Arts of Isfahan* [New York, 1973], no. 53). We are indebted to Annemarie Schimmel for the translation.

PUBLISHED: Stuart C. Welch, *Wonders of the Age* (Cambridge, 1979), no. 75.

## 50 / A Family of Cheetahs
Attrib. to Basawan
India; ca. 1575–1580
Page: H. 40.1 cm., W. 27.1 cm.
Miniature: H. 29.5 cm., W. 18.5 cm.

Most Muslim painting was on paper, intended for inclusion in precious manuscripts or albums. The number of paintings on cloth—either cotton (as here) or silk—is small, and most were produced under Mughal patronage early in Akbar's reign, when the immense *Hamzanamah* (originally containing fourteen hundred very large pictures) was completed. This painting of a cheetah family however, never illustrated a manuscript but was done as a single picture, almost certainly for the delectation or amusement of the emperor Akbar.

Animal studies—in this case a real group portrait—were a Mughal specialty, here combined with the closest observation of the natural setting. Shaded by a gnarled and twisted tree and protected by rocky knolls, the family rests in a grassy glade. Behind the tree glows a golden sky, streaked blue at the top of the page. In keeping with the Mughal interest in the here-and-now, it is a world examined and recorded, rather than transformed to grace, in art. It is also imbued with wry observation and gentle humor. The father of the young family is smug; his smile and relaxed, crossed-paws posture project great self-contentment. The mother is busy, washing one cub and nursing another while two more cubs romp in the grass. Most Mughal paintings of cheetahs reflect their use in the hunt: they are shown either during capture or as trained (and collared) coursers. This kind of family idyll is a rarity.

The painting is closest in style and spirit to a 1570 manuscript of the *Anvar-i Suhayli* (see cat. no. 32 for a discussion of the text)[1] and to a circa 1575 portrait of a cow and her calf that has been attributed to Basawan, the painter perhaps most responsible for the development of classical Mughal painting.[2] Its soft contours, imaginative nuances of color, and sensitivity to emotions and personalities mark *A Family of Cheetahs* as his work.[3] The painting, which must have delighted the royal patron, was subsequently mounted on gold-sprinkled paper and bound in an album.

A. W.

1. In the possession of the School of Oriental and African Studies, University of London; pages from the manuscript are reproduced in most studies of Mughal painting, including Douglas Barrett and Basil Gray, *Painting of India* (Lausanne, 1963; reprint ed., New York, 1978), p. 80; and Stuart C. Welch, *Imperial Mughal Painting* (New York, 1978), pl. 4.
2. This attribution is the suggestion of Stuart C. Welch. For his monograph on Basawan, see "The Paintings of Basawan," *Lalit Kala* 10 (1961); for the *Cow and Calf,* see idem, *Imperial*

**50** / (also in color)

*Mughal Painting,* fig. 3; in the same work pls. 8, 12, and 13 reproduce other paintings by Basawan.

3. Abu'l-Fazl knew Basawan's work well and discusses him in the *A'in-i Akbari,* 1:114: "In backgrounding, drawing of features, distribution of colors, portrait painting, and several other branches, he is most excellent. . . ."

## 51 / Babur Racing with Qasim Beg and Qambar ʿAli
Attrib. to Mitra
India; ca. 1590
From a manuscript of the *Baburnamah*
Page: H. 26.6 cm., W. 15.7 cm.
Miniature: H. 21.6 cm., W. 13.5 cm.

Shortly after the transfer of his capital from Fathpur Sikri to Lahore in 1586, Akbar began commissioning splendidly illustrated manuscripts of Islamic histories and of the memoirs of his dynastic predecessors. Among the very first of these books was the *Baburnamah* (the *Memoirs* of his grandfather, Babur, the first Mughal emperor), translated from its original Chaghatai Turkish into Persian by Akbar's learned general, the Khan Khanan ʿAbd al-Rahim ibn Bairam Khan.[1] Akbar's own copy was completed in 1589 (A.H. 998), and several others were finished about the same time.[2] The *Baburnamah* is one of the great memoirs in world literature. Keenly ambitious but with a refreshing sense of objectivity about himself, Babur suffered multiple setbacks in his ultimately unsuccessful struggle with the Uzbeks for control of Samarqand and his perceived Central Asian patrimony; but from his base in the city of Kabul he led a coalition of forces against the Lodi sultans of Delhi in 1526 and with a series of victories laid the basis for the Mughal empire. Neither privation nor success altered his fundamentally resilient character and his open-eyed sense of wonder and appreciation for the world around him. Written near the end of his life from notes composed in earlier years, his *Memoirs* served as a kind of dynastic standard for his descendants on the Mughal throne.

This page probably comes from a dispersed manuscript of the *Baburnamah*.[3] On the reverse are eleven lines of text that describe Babur's departure from Samarqand after surrendering it to the Uzbek leader Shaybani Khan in 1501. Despite the bitter loss of the city and the imminent danger surrounding him and his mere one hundred followers, his natural ebullience took over the next day, and he impetuously raced two of his friends:

> From the north slope of Qara-bugh we hurried on past the foot of Juduk village and dropped down into Yilan-auti. On the road I raced with Qasim Beg and Qambar-ʿAli (the Skinner); my horse was leading when I, thinking to look at theirs behind, twisted myself round; the girth may have

من گذشت بجهت دیدن اسپان ایشان که چه مقدار

عقب مانده اند خم شده برگشته دیدم تک اسپ خود کند

51 /

slackened, for my saddle turned and I was thrown on my head to the ground. Although I at once got up and remounted, my brain did not steady till the evening; till then this world and what went on appeared to me like things felt and seen in a dream or fancy.4

In the illustration, Babur, dressed in orange and mounted on a blue horse, is shown just as he turns in his saddle to estimate his lead and as his friends and various followers, apparently spotting the loose girth, gesture to him. Though the text mentions a village, the painting shows a distant walled city.

Commencing with the *Baburnamah,* it became general practice in the Mughal atelier to add the painter's name in the lower part of his painting. In the lower right is a pale red ascription to the artist Mitra, who is not mentioned in the *A'in-i Akbari.*

A. W.

1. The first Persian translation of the *Baburnamah* was apparently prepared during Babur's lifetime by his religious official and poet Shaykh Zayn al-Din Khwafi. Perhaps due to the ornate style of this translation, a second one in a plainer style was completed some years later for one of Akbar's military officers, Nawrang Khan, who considered it incumbent on every Mughal adherent to know the book. The third translation, by the Khan Khanan, has remained the most widely known and read.

2. Akbar's 1589 copy of the *Baburnamah* is in the British Museum, Add. 24,416. Other copies are in the Walters Art Gallery, Baltimore; the Museum of Oriental Art, Moscow; and the National Museum of India, New Delhi.

3. It cannot come from either the Moscow or New Delhi manuscripts, since in both of them the same scene a moment later is illustrated, showing Babur already tumbled off his horse. Another page from the dispersed *Baburnamah* is also in the Sadruddin Aga Khan Collection and shows the successful attack of Babur's troops on the inhabitants of Bilah.

4. *The Babur-nama in English,* trans. Annette S. Beveridge, from the original Turki text (London, 1922), p. 147.

## 52 / Humayun Defeats Kamran at Kabul

India; ca. 1595–1600
From a manuscript of the *Akbarnamah*
Page: H. 36.9 cm., W. 25.2 cm.
Miniature: H. 32.8 cm., W. 21.1 cm.

Two of our major sources of information about the Mughal emperor Akbar (r. 1556–1605) were written by his boon companion and adviser Abu'l-Fazl. The *A'in-i Akbari* provides encyclopedic information about late sixteenth-century India and Mughal administration; the *Akbarnamah* is directly concerned with Akbar's life and career. The *Akbarnamah* also deals with Akbar's father, Humayun, who was overcome by Sher Shah in 1540 and subsequently driven out of India to a brief exile in Iran. He did not regain the Mughal throne until 1555. Humayun's brother, Mirza Kamran,

entrusted with the important governorship of Kabul, consistently betrayed Humayun. Often indecisive and for many years unwilling to punish Kamran, Humayun finally defeated him in 1550 outside Kabul and a few days later ordered him to be blinded.

Akbar commissioned at least two copies of the *Akbarnamah*.[1] One volume of the earlier and larger manuscript is in the Victoria and Albert Museum; produced between 1595 and 1600 by the major artists in Akbar's employ, it is the finest of his historical manuscripts. A number of detached leaves that originally belonged to this *Akbarnamah* are in other collections;[2] in size, style, and marginal notations *Humayun Defeats Kamran* is obviously one of these. It would originally have illustrated chapter 48.

An inscription in the lower left of this page identifies the battle. Kabul is shown in the upper left. From the upper right the Mughal army winds around rocky formations to the center, where Humayun in golden armor on a brilliantly caparisoned horse leads the troops pursuing Kamran's defeated forces. The painting's dramatic perspective is derived from European prints, but the bloody realism and sense of terror in the fleeing soldiers is akin to the style of the earlier *Hamzanamah*, one of the first books produced by Akbar's atelier. A second red inscription at the bottom of the page ascribes the picture mostly to Mahesh, who also painted several other illustrations in this *Akbarnamah*, but states that certain faces were rendered by Padarath.[3]

A. W.

1. The volume in the Victoria and Albert Museum contains 117 paintings. The second *Akbarnamah*, produced between 1602 and 1610, is divided between the Chester Beatty Library, Dublin, the British Library, and numerous other collections. See cat. no. 64 for further references. Akbar also commissioned royal manuscripts of the memoirs of his grandfather Babur and his ancestor Timur.

2. Other pages are in the India Office Library, London; the Freer Gallery of Art, Washington, D.C.; the Cleveland Museum of Art; the Los Angeles County Museum of Art; and the collection of Edwin Binney, 3rd.

3. Mahesh is cited by Abu'l-Fazl in chap. 34 of the *A'in-i Akbari* as a major contemporary painter. Padarath is known to have worked on the Beatty *Akbarnamah*.

PUBLISHED: Stuart C. Welch, "Early Mughal Miniature Paintings from Two Private Collections," *Ars Orientalis* 3 (1959):138, fig. 7.

## 53 / The Munificence of Jaʿfar al-Baramaki to ʿAbd al-Malik

India; ca. 1595
From a manuscript of the *Akhbar-i Barmakiyan*
Page: H. 27.7 cm., W. 19.7 cm.
Miniature: H. 22 cm., W. 12.7 cm.

Akbar's interest in instructive histories was responsible for an illustrated copy of the *Akhbar-i Barmakiyan* (Traditions of the Barmecids), made either

شوانم گذارد

عبدالملک هاشمی گفت مرا جهار حاجت بر در تو آورده ست یکی آنکه صد هزار درم و وام دارم ملکی بسیطیم که محصول آن

دویست هزار درم باشد از اخراجات اشیاع و اطباع فراغ حاصل شود و هر سال وام برهنا بید و سیوم دختر

خلیفه را بخواهم جهت احمد پسر خود حسن جعفر ثبت است او شنید خواست تا ببلغ مال از خاصه خودبش عبدالملک آرد

53

on his orders or as a gift for him by another patron. The text is less a formal history than a compilation of anecdotes demonstrating generosity in high places. The original ninth-century Arabic text had been translated into Persian in the fourteenth century by the Muslim Indian scholar Ziya al-Din Barani, who served under the Tughluq sultans Muhammad (r. 1325–1351) and Firuz Shah (r. 1351–1388).[1] As its guiding principle is didactic, it may be included in that class of Persian literature known as "mirrors for princes," which had been written since the tenth century to instruct rulers in proper princely behavior.[2] If the patron of this manuscript was not royal, he may have hoped that the book's message would elicit a favorable royal response.[3]

The two protagonists in this illustration are well-known figures in ninth-century 'Abbasid history. A distant cousin of the caliph Harun al-Rashid (r. 786–806), 'Abd al-Malik al-Hashimi was imprisoned in 803 after having served as governor in Medina and in Egypt. Ja'far al-Baramaki, younger son of the brilliant *vazir* Yahya ibn Khalid al-Baramaki, was celebrated for his elegant diction and his knowledge of Islamic law. As a great favorite of Harun al-Rashid, he was given positions of distinction, being at various times governor, director of the mint, and tutor to Prince al-Ma'mun. Eventually the Barmecids' vast wealth and power aroused the caliph's distrust, and in 803 Ja'far was executed and the caliph moved into his former friend's palace in Baghdad.

In this painting Ja'far sits at the left listening to 'Abd al-Malik, who not only owes him money but is requesting further funds for his son, Ahmad, engaged to the caliph's daughter. Ja'far prudently forgives him the debt and promises him the loan he needs. Its thin colors and straightforward, unadorned style make it unlikely that this page was painted by major artists in Akbar's atelier. If there were once any attributions below the picture, they have been lost in later trimming and remounting, for at some point the manuscript was dismembered and this leaf put in an album.[4] Its reverse now displays seven *nasta'liq* lines from a moralizing poem, perhaps Sa'di's *Bustan*.

A. W.

1. Barani is best known for his important history of the Delhi sultanate between the years 1266 and 1357 (*Tarikh-i Firuz Shahi*), which was similarly didactic in purpose.

2. A complete text of the *Akhbar-i Barmakiyan* is in the British Museum, Or. 151 (Charles Rieu, *Catalogue of the Persian Manuscripts in the British Museum* [London, 1879], 1:333–34).

3. Edwin Binney, 3rd, *Indian Miniature Painting, The Mughal and Deccani Schools* (Portland, Ore., 1973), p. 39, has published two pages from this manuscript. He concludes that it was "prepared for a non-royal patron."

4. A second page from this manuscript is in Prince Sadruddin's collection and will be published in a forthcoming volume of the catalogue.

## 54 / Mourning the Death of Abaqa

By Makund and Bhanwari
India; ca. 1596–1600
From a manuscript of the *Jami' al-Tawarikh*
Page: H. 36.6 cm., W. 24.6 cm.
Miniature: H. 30.8 cm., W. 20.3 cm.

As he expanded his state militarily and consolidated it administratively, Akbar employed artists to produce impressive copies of dynastically relevant books. Among them were not only the predictable Mughal dynastic memoirs, such as the *Baburnamah* and the *Akbarnamah,* but also more purely historical works, such as the *Jami' al-Tawarikh* (World History). This was composed by the Il-Khan (Mongol) *vazir* of Iran, Rashid al-Din, in Tabriz early in the fourteenth century. Though the World History presented human history from Creation through the Mongol conquest of the Near East, Akbar commissioned only the last sections, dealing with the history of the Mongols in Iran.[1] The Timurids, the great Muslim dynastic clan to which the Mughals belonged, claimed descent from the Mongols, and the emperor's interest in Mongol history therefore conforms to the Mughal interest in genealogies and histories that supported their royal descent and resultant right to rule.

The second Il-Khan monarch, Abaqa (r. 1265–1282), strengthened and organized the state he had inherited from his father, Hulagu. A Buddhist, and tolerant of Christians, Abaqa pursued policies in some ways parallel to those of Akbar, who may therefore have found Abaqa's portion of the *History* especially interesting. In a setting resembling sixteenth-century Mughal architecture, Abaqa is mourned by Muslims and Mongols with a fervor that seems to derive pictorially from fourteenth-century Iranian painting.[2]

The copying of the text was completed on 25 May 1596, and the miniatures were added over the ensuing several years. Although a number of pages have entered private collections in recent years,[3] the largest part of the manuscript is in the Gulistan Library, Tehran, part of the booty brought back by Nadir Shah after his sack of Delhi in 1739. It was a product of Akbar's atelier of the time when the classic Mughal style had come to fruition and when dozens of artists were employed producing manuscripts ranging from the delicate sensitivity of the *Diwan* of Shahi (see cat. no. 59) to more quickly rendered and visually simpler works like the *Jami' al-Tawarikh.* Below the illustration is recorded precise librarian's information about its production: "Drawn by Makund and painted by Bhanwari the elder," well-known artists somewhat below the stature of Basawan, La'l, and Mansur, who also contributed illustrations to the manuscript.

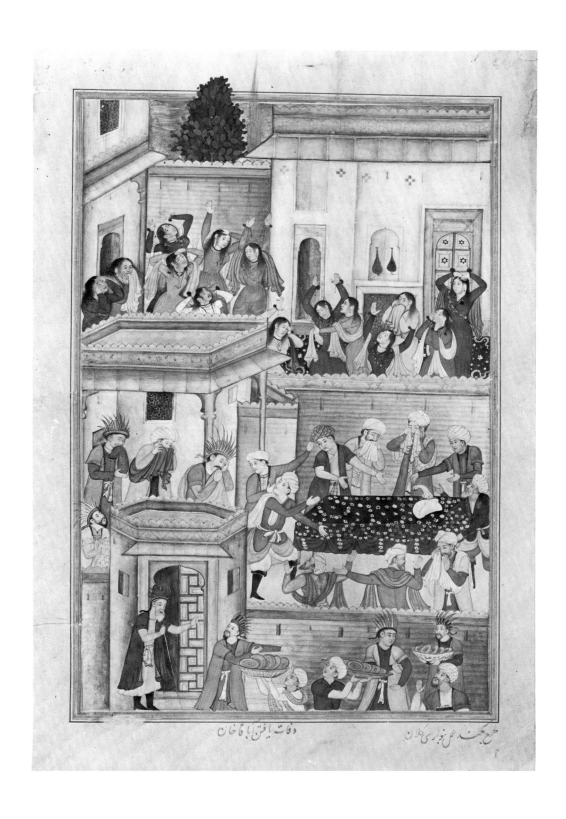

On the reverse are seventeen horizontal and ten diagonal lines of text in a good *nastaʿliq* hand.

A. W.

1. This is apparently the text referred to by Abu'l-Fazl as the *Chingiznamah* (see Abu'l-Fazl, *The Aʾin-i Akbari*, trans. H. Blochmann, 2nd ed. [Calcutta, 1927], p. 114).

2. E.g., the "Mourning for Isfandiyar" from the Demotte *Shahnamah*, reproduced in Oleg Grabar and Sheila Blair, *Epic Images and Contemporary History* (Chicago, 1980), p. 101.

3. See Sotheby's sale catalogue, London, 14 October 1980, lot 240.

## 55 / A Prince and a Hermit

Attrib. to ʿAbd al-Samad
India; ca. 1585–1590
Page: H. 39.6 cm., W. 31.3 cm.
Miniature: H. 34.5 cm., W. 22.8 cm.

Themes resonant in Iranian literature and art have been translated here for an Indian patron, either the Mughal emperor Akbar or his son Prince Salim. The mighty stallion, in Iran a symbol of worldly pomp and power (and, by the same token, of worldly impermanence), dominates the lower half of the page as he dominates the five servants, who hover around the prince's steed as they would around his master. The prince, however, sits beneath a plane tree, talking with a hermit whose flimsy mantle emphasizes his extreme emaciation. Wild animals are gathered trustingly around him, and what might have been a royal hunt has been transformed into a peaceable kingdom by the holy man's protective presence. A major theme in Iranian culture, the meeting of high aristocrat and humble dervish (or hermit) presents the fleeting juxtaposition and distant affinity of temporal and spiritual authority, reflected here even in the prince's eight sleek servants and the hermit's single wraithlike disciple. The birds in the painting embody the hermit's goal: they are "souls set free." The rocks, meanwhile, have been endowed with animal or human features (a heavy-set and bulbous-nosed individual stares perplexed over the hermit's left shoulder), making of the natural setting an animate world—a conception and a treatment common in Iranian painting since the fourteenth century.

Yet despite its Iranian themes, this is an Indian painting, its Persian elegance and grace amplified by the figural fullness, naturalism, and sense of depth characteristic of Mughal painting. Indicative of the artistic synthesis created under Akbar's patronage, the painting can be confidently attributed to ʿAbd al-Samad (perhaps working with a gifted assistant), one of the Safavid Iranian masters who left Shah Tahmasp's court in Qazvin to work first under Humayun and then under Akbar.[1] A well-known passage

from Abu'l-Fazl's *A'in-i Akbari* reveals the effect of Akbar's patronage on 'Abd al-Samad's art:

> Khwaja 'Abd al-Samad, styled Shirinqalam, or Sweet Pen. He comes from Shiraz. Though he had learnt the art before he was made a grandee of the court, his perfection was mainly due to the wonderful effect of a look of His Majesty, which caused him to turn from that which is form to that which is spirit.[2]

Miniatures from the Mughal phase of this artist's career are well known and support this attribution on stylistic grounds, revealing the same two-tiered composition, rocky formations, and figural types found in this painting.[3] Catalogue number 56 in this volume, which is virtually identical in theme and style with the picture under discussion, not only bears the name of 'Abd al-Samad but also identifies the seated prince as Akbar's son, Salim. The young aristocrats in the two paintings are similar enough to suggest that the attentive but unnamed Mughal in this present painting may also be Prince Salim, the future emperor Jahangir.

Although the miniature may once have illustrated a poetic manuscript, it was subsequently mounted in an album, and on its reverse is now an unsigned calligraphy: three lines in the *thuluth* style of script, beginning with the *bismillah* (the Qur'an's first words) and continuing in Arabic with a pious warning.

A. W.

1. This attribution has been proposed by Stuart C. Welch. For 'Abd al-Samad and the formation of the Mughal school of painting, see Martin B. Dickson and Stuart C. Welch, *The Houghton Shahnameh* (Cambridge, Mass., 1981), especially pp. 192–200, 118–28, 178–91.

2. Abu'l-Fazl, *The A'in-i Akbari*, 2nd ed. (Calcutta, 1927), 1:114.

3. For paintings by 'Abd al-Samad, see Dickson and Welch, *Houghton Shahnameh*.

## 56 / Prince Salim and a Dervish

By 'Abd al-Samad
India; ca. 1586–1587
Page: H. 39 cm., W. 25.4 cm.
Miniature: H. 23 cm., W. 16 cm.

*Nim qalam* (half-pen), the technique of lightly tinting parts of a drawing, is excellently demonstrated in this picture. The meeting of a prince and a dervish is a frequent theme in Islamic literature and art, but the meeting depicted here may well have taken place, for Prince Salim (the future emperor Jahangir) was not only more committed to Islam than his father Akbar but was also interested in Sufis and hermits. As in the two other such encounters depicted in this collection, the elaborate hunt has come to

56 / Reverse

a halt and the erstwhile prey look on in peace, protected by the holy presence, who may belong to the Khaksar dervish, an order that developed in India.[1] A rocky mound fills the upper right distance; a *chinar* (plane tree) fills the upper left, and below it on a throne-like mound sits the prince, while the dervish stands, appropriately on a smaller mound. His horn, his *kashkul* (beggar's bowl), and his garb identify him unmistakably as a dervish. At the right is a short inscription of great importance: "The son of the emperor Akbar; the work of ʿAbd al-Samad Shirin Qalam."

Both rocks and *chinar* identify the landscape as Kashmir, which had just been conquered by the Mughals. Born in 1569, the heir to the Mughal throne would have been seventeen or eighteen years old here, and the inscription naming him as "Akbar's son" rather than "Salim"[2] suggests that the drawing was made for the emperor, not the prince. It is, of course, a very literary portrait, incorporating the young prince into a conceit that any literate Muslim would have understood. This meeting contrasts worldly and otherworldly, earthly and spiritual wealth. There is a single dervish but many courtiers; the animals, though protected by the holy man's attendance, still direct their glances at the prince. The goat even kneels. In keeping with Akbar's elevated concept of Mughal kingship, the two do not meet on equal terms: the dervish supplicates, the prince deigns to grant.

ʿAbd al-Samad, the artist, had been styled Shirin Qalam (Sweet Pen) by Akbar, and Abu'l-Fazl's appreciation of his art is quoted elsewhere.[3] He followed several careers in his long life and flourished in all of them. He had been trained in the Iranian capital of Tabriz under Shah Tahmasp, and one picture in the great Houghton *Shahnamah* (fol. 742b), produced for that king in the first half of his reign, is attributable to him. In 1546 the Mughal emperor Humayun invited him to follow him east, and in 1549 he did so. He was known for calligraphy as well as painting, and since he gave instruction to both Humayun and Akbar, he may also have taught Prince Salim. An orthodox Muslim, he was apparently a Shiʿa, and Akbar's official (and clandestine historian) Badaoni, a pious Sunni, did not entirely approve:

> (Khwajah ʿAbd al-Samad of Shiraz) . . . is much occupied with ceremonial prayers and fasts, and with supererogatory prayers and outward devotions, and had great faith in the Haji; he (the Haji Ibrahim the Traditionist) used to say, "Khwajah, all these observances will profit you nothing until you give a place in your heart to love for the orthodox successors of the prophet."[4]

Akbar gave the artist a *mansab* (honorary command, i.e., a sinecure) of four hundred troops, and in 1578 the emperor placed him in charge of the mint at Fathpur Sikri, a powerful and lucrative post. Later in his career he was given authority over the city of Multan. Such power granted to an artist (who was celebrated for his pious, not-to-say miraculous, calligraphies on grains of rice and poppy seeds) is indicative of the often close relationships between Mughal rulers and members of their ateliers.[5]

In this drawing, executed when 'Abd al-Samad must have been well advanced in years, his Iranian origins are only dimly perceptible. Such passages as the roundly modeled, particularly expressive horses' heads and the lively dogs suggest that he may have been assisted by Basawan, another major Mughal artist. It was during this period that the young prince Salim began to emerge as a sensitive patron of painting and calligraphy, and the inscription at the right may be the artist's acknowledgment of their student-teacher relationship.[6]

A gold floral inner border was added around the drawing when it was mounted as an album page, probably during the reign of Shah Jahan. The outer margins, replete with flying birds, deer, gazelles, and a hunting cheetah, were added at the same time: they are the work of a follower of the Master of the Borders.[7]

It is the Master of the Borders himself who is responsible for the superb floral margins on the reverse, where tulips and other flowers sway and bow in the gentlest of winds. Their long, bent leaves and palpable sense of life typify his style. The inner borders—in plain gold, green with gold arabesque, and pale tan with gold arabesque—were all pasted on when the page was composed. The calligraphy on the reverse consists of two parts. The twelve small panels that form the innermost border contain love verses by the late fifteenth-century Iranian poet Jami, whose name is mentioned in one of the final passages. The calligraphy in the large central panel, illuminated with tiny flowers and thin arabesque against a gold background, reads as follows:

> From my master Mir 'Ali, may his grave be
>   illumined.[8]
> From the time that my heart became inflicted
>   with that honey-lipped one,
> Neither day nor night is there peace for me.
> From night to dawn I weep blood because
>   of her separation,
> And every day I ask more than a hundred
>   times for my death.
> Written by the sinful poor man, 'Abd al-Rahim
>   'Anbarin Qalam.

While still a young man, 'Abd al-Rahim left his native city of Herat (where his cited master Mir 'Ali, who could not have trained him, had lived) for India and entered the service of the Khan Khanan, Akbar's highest official. He later worked for Jahangir, who gave him the *khitab* (epithet) 'Anbarin Qalam (Amber Pen). Dated calligraphies by his hand range from 1591 to 1625.[9] These include a 1624–1625 copy of the *Jahangirnamah* in the former royal library, Tehran, and the 1595–1596 copy of Nizami's *Khamsah* in the British Museum, in which we find below the final colophon a double portrait of the calligrapher ʿAbd al-Rahim and the painter Daulat, dated to 1609.[10]

A. W.

1. Cat. nos. 55 and 59 deal with this theme. We are indebted to Annemarie Schimmel for the suggestion that the dervish may belong to the Khaksar order.

2. He is identified as Shah Salim in a 1599 *nim qalam* drawn during one of his revolts against Akbar (see cat. no. 60).

3. See cat. no. 55.

4. al-Badaoni, *Muntakhabu-t-Tawarikh*, trans. T. W. Haig (Calcutta, 1899), 3:196. Shiʿas ritually denounce the first three caliphs as usurpers.

5. The above discussion of ʿAbd al-Samad is heavily dependent upon the analysis of that artist in Martin B. Dickson and Stuart C. Welch, *The Houghton Shahnameh* (Cambridge, Mass., 1981). The artist's son was also a painter, poet, and calligrapher, whom Badaoni (*Muntakhabu*, pp. 429–30) praises: "His name is Sharif, and he is the son of Khwajaha ʿAbd al-Samad, the painter. He is a youth lately come to man's estate, and he is unrivalled in beauty of penmanship and in painting. It is well known that his father wrote in full, and in a good and legible hand, on one side of a poppy seed, the *Surah al-Ikhlas,* and on the other side of it the argument of the chapter; and they say that his son, Sharif, bored in one poppy seed eight small holes, and passed wires through them, and that he drew, on a grain of rice, a picture of an armed horseman, preceded by an outrider, and bearing all the things proper to a horseman such as a sword, a shield, a polo stick, etc. Sharif has a pleasant nature. He has composed a *diwan* and the following verses were selected by him from his works and given to me (for insertion in this work)."

6. Stuart C. Welch, whose study of Basawan is cited in cat. no. 50, n. 2, proposed that he assisted the Iranian master in this picture. For the suggestion that Prince Salim (later Emperor Jahangir) was an eager, influential patron as early as the 1580s, see Annemarie Schimmel and Stuart C. Welch, *A Pocketbook for Akbar* (New York, forthcoming).

7. See cat. no. 72 for observations upon the Master of the Borders.

8. The reference is presumably to Mir ʿAli al-Haravi, who had learned his art under Sultan ʿAli Mashhadi and who died in Bukhara about 1544. For further information on Mir ʿAli, see Anthony Welch, *Calligraphy in the Arts of the Muslim World* (Austin and London, 1979), no. 83.

9. ʿAbd al-Rahim al-Haravi ʿAnbarin Qalam also wrote cat. no. 64, a closely related small *Bustan* of Saʿdi, and a number of other manuscripts (probably including cat. no. 59). Mehdi Bayani, *Kushnevisan* [Calligraphers] (Tehran, 1966), 2:389–91, discusses the scribe and lists thirteen of his signed works.

10. See A. K. Das, *Mughal Painting during Jahangir's Time* (Calcutta, 1978), p. 59 and pl. 9. This double portrait of calligrapher and painter parallels the double portrait of Muhammad Hasan Zarin Qalam and Manohar, discussed in cat. no. 57, n. 8.

PUBLISHED: S. C. Welch, *Indian Drawings and Painted Sketches* (New York, 1976), no. 10, where further aspects of this drawing are discussed.

**57 / Flight of a *Simurgh***
Attrib. to Basawan
India; ca. 1590
Page: H. 38.8 cm., W. 25.2 cm.
Miniature: H. 32.8 cm., W. 21 cm.

A Muslim arriving at Akbar's court from Iran or Central Asia would have recognized this picture immediately: the phoenix-like giant *simurgh* plays

**57** / (also in color)

**57** / Reverse

an important role in the epic and mystical literatures of Arabs, Turks, and Iranians, though it receives here a more "naturalistic" rendering than it would have had from a Safavid or Ottoman artist.[1]

But if he knew his Persian texts well, our observer might have been puzzled. The Persian poet Nizami's *Haft Paykar* is constructed around King Bahram Gur's seven wives, each of whom comes from a different part of the world, lives in a differently colored pavilion, and tells him a different tale on one day of the week. The Indian princess begins the book, and the hero of her story at one point escapes from bondage and arrives in a paradisaical land by clinging to the feet of a *simurgh*. That is what we see here, except that the text does not mention the *simurgh*'s meal, apparently added by the artist.[2] Whether this superb picture was ever included in a *Haft Paykar* for Akbar is not known.[3] About 1635 it was bound in a suitably royal album for Akbar's grandson, Shah Jahan.

The painting shows a peninsula or island whose water margins are filled with aquatic creatures. The land itself is lush: soft green grass, blossoms, and dark green trees with a small white temple nestled discreetly among them at the right. A multihued mountain rises into a subtly modulated blue sky at the left, while at the right the *simurgh* rises in the air. Two hapless men are clutched in its beak; the hero of the tale grips its feet. At the top of the miniature is the ascription "Basawan," perhaps Akbar's greatest painter; the sense of tangible volume, the prevailing softness of figures and receding landscape, and the sensitive and sympathetic observation all corroborate this attribution.[4]

The page's floral arabesque border, cruelly trimmed, appears to be the work of Shah Jahan's great, as-yet-unidentified illuminator, whom we refer to here as the Master of the Borders.[5] He is also responsible for the elegant floral border framing the calligraphy on the reverse: its perfect blossoms bend in a stately visual minuet. The margins were prepared about 1635, when the album was produced for Shah Jahan.

The calligraphy on the reverse consists of two parts. Fourteen small panels, comprising an inner border, contain lines from an unidentified heroic epic in the meter of Firdausi's *Shahnamah;* they were put in place when the album was constructed. The large inner rectangle presents an Arabic prayer, filled with Qur'anic expressions written in a masterful hand by Muhammad Husayn Zarin Qalam (Golden Pen), one of the greatest Mughal calligraphers, whose name appears in minute script in the lower left. Born, like Akbar, about 1542, Muhammad Husayn flourished at the Mughal court and was greatly admired by Abu'l-Fazl (among others), who discusses him at some length in the *A'in-i Akbari:*

> His Majesty shows much regard to the art (of calligraphy) and takes a great interest in the different systems of writing; hence the large number of

skillful calligraphists. *Nasta'liq* has especially received a new impetus. The artist who, in the shadow of the throne of his Majesty, has become a master of calligraphy is Muhammad Husayn of Kashmir. He has been honored with the title of Zarin Qalam, the gold pen. He surpassed his master, Mawlana 'Abd al-'Aziz; his *maddat* and *dawa'ir* show everywhere a proper proportion to each other, and art critics consider him equal to Mulla Mir 'Ali.[6]

Like his equally great colleague 'Abd al-Rahim 'Anbarin Qalam,[7] Muhammad Husayn copied a number of great Mughal manuscripts; he was also celebrated as a teacher of his art.[8]

A. W.

1. For a brief discussion of the *simurgh,* see cat. no. 29 and Anthony Welch, *Calligraphy in the Arts of the Muslim World* (Austin and London, 1979), no. 83.

2. In the Sanskrit collection of animal fables, the *Katha-Sarit-Sagara* [*Ocean of the Streams of Story*], trans. C. H. Tawney (Calcutta, 1880), there are several tales involving *simurghs* and human beings that may have influenced the artist's conception of this scene.

3. Akbar's 1595–1596 *Khamsah* of Nizami (British Museum Or. 1220) illustrates this incident with greater fidelity to the text. (See Frederick R. Martin, *The Miniature Paintings and Painters of Persia, India, and Turkey* [London, 1912], p. 180.)

4. For another painting by Basawan and relevant bibliography on the artist, see cat. no. 50.

5. See cat. no. 72 for a discussion of this illuminator. Cat. nos. 56, 62, 65, and 73 also show work by his hand.

6. Abu'l-Fazl, *A'in-i Akbari,* trans. H. Blochmann, 2nd ed. (Calcutta, 1927) 1:109.

7. For works by and discussion of 'Abd al-Rahim, see cat. nos. 56, 58, 59.

8. A well-known painting portrays Muhammad Husayn instructing Basawan's son Manohar in calligraphy (reproduced in Welch, *Calligraphy,* no. 76, where the scribe is also discussed). A more extensive presentation of the calligrapher and his work is to be found in Mehdi Bayani, *Khushnevisan* [Calligraphers] (Tehran, 1966), 3:702–4.

## 58 / A Manuscript of the *Akhlaq-i Nasiri*

India, Lahore; ca. 1590–1595
H. 23.7 cm., W. 14.3 cm.

Although not a reader, Akbar was a passionate learner with a wide range of interests and a superb memory. He commissioned manuscripts not only because he loved pictures but also because he loved the texts, and Abu'l-Fazl's *A'in-i Akbari* gives a vivid impression of the content and process of his continuing education:

Experienced people bring (these books) daily and read them before his Majesty, who hears every book from the beginning to the end. At whatever page the readers daily stop, his Majesty makes with his own pen a sign, according to the number of pages; and rewards the readers with presents of cash, either in gold or silver, according to the number of leaves read out by them. Among books of renown, there are few that are not read in his Majesty's assembly hall; and there are no historical facts of the past

**58** / folio 137a: Horsemanship

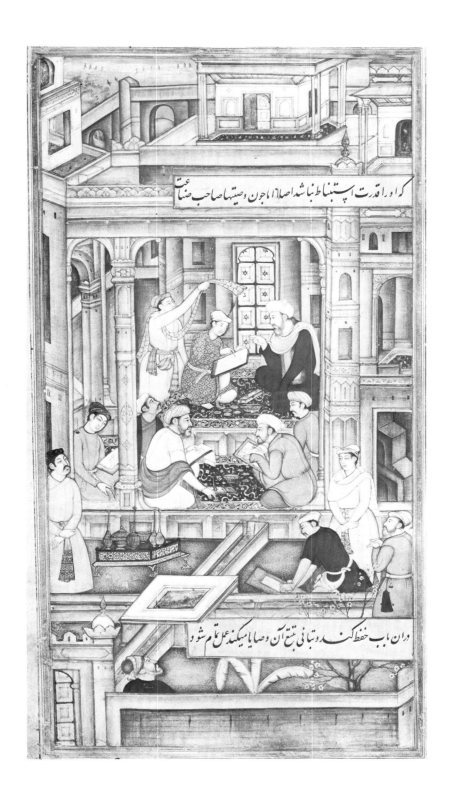

**58** / folio 196a: A manuscript atelier

ages, or curiosities of science, or interesting points of philosophy, with which his Majesty, a leader of impartial sages, is unacquainted. He does not get tired of hearing a book over again, but listens to the reading of it with more interest. The *Akhlaq-i Nasiri*, . . . the *Gulistan*, . . . the *Bustan*, the *Shahnamah*, the collected *masnavis* of Shaykh Nizami, the works of Khusraw and Mawlana Jami, . . . and several works on history, are continually read out to his Majesty.[1]

Abu'l-Fazl takes care to cite the *Akhlaq-i Nasiri* (*The Nasirean Ethics*), a philosophical and ethical treatise that Akbar valued highly. The original text was commissioned by Nasir al-Din 'Abd al-Rahim, the Isma'ili governor of Quhistan, and completed about 1235 by Nasir al-Din Tusi (1201–1274), a philosopher, scientist, and man of letters who was one of the great intellects of medieval Iran.[2] He remained in Isma'ili employ until 1247, when he left to serve the invading Mongols under Hulagu. His *Akhlaq-i Nasiri* is divided into three discourses, dealing with ethics, social rights and regulations, and political theory and practice.

This manuscript consists of 254 pages written in an elegant *nasta'liq;* there is no colophon identifying the scribe, but the hand would appear to be that of 'Abd al-Rahim 'Anbarin Qalam, one of Akbar's most celebrated and prolific scribes.[3] The initial page has an illuminated *'unwan* (title cartouche), and the manuscript is illustrated with seventeen full-page miniatures that stylistically belong to the period from about 1590 to 1595, when Akbar's court atelier at Lahore was extremely active.[4] Though some of the pages have been trimmed and remounted, others still bear notations about the artists, and those named—Kanak Singh, Dhanraj, Tulsi Kalan, Phim Gujarati, Sajnu, Khim Karan, and Nand—are known to have been in Akbar's employ. Their work here is consistent with their painting in other manuscripts of the period.[5]

The task of illustrating a philosophical treatise could not have been easy. Lacking episodes, leading figures, or established iconography, the *Nasirean Ethics* did not provide a ready visual subject matter, and the business of creating suitable pictorial content must have been delegated to an intellectual like Abu'l-Fazl. The inherent difficulty of the task can be seen from the text for folio 137a (illustrated):

> Crafts are of three kinds, noble, base, and intermediate. Noble crafts are those coming within the range of the soul, not that of the body; and they are called the crafts of liberal men and of the polite. The greater part of them come within three classes; that which is dependent on the substance of the intelligence, such as sound opinion, apposite counsel, and good management—and this is the craft of ministers; that which is dependent on cultivation and learning, such as writing and rhetoric, astrology and medicine, accounting and surveying—and this is the craft of men of letters and of culture; and that which is dependent on strength and courage, such

as horsemanship, military command, the control of frontiers and the re-pulsion of enemies—and this is the craft of chivalry.[6]

Only in the final sentence is the picture's content—horsemanship—actually mentioned. This particular scene was chosen, presumably as a generic reference to chivalry, and because its iconography was established in the illustration of epics, romances, and histories. But as clarification of the text, it is all but pointless: the illustration is there for its own sake, as a piece of fine painting. It is signed by Kanak Singh, a painter strongly influenced by Farrukh Chela.[7]

Similarly, folio 196a (illustrated) is a representation of an active manuscript atelier: a master supervises a scribe, while two painters, a second scribe, and a paper maker are at work. It "illustrates" a section dealing with social strata and urban organization. Among the several classes are the communications specialists, who bridge the gap between the rulers and the ruled: "Their craft comprises the sciences of Scholastics, Jurisprudence, Elocution, Rhetoric, Poetry, and Calligraphy."[8] The painting bears the name Sajnu, written in a very rough hand.

Most of the manuscript's miniatures deal with crafts, arts, and professions, the kinds of occupations that Abu'l-Fazl was careful to describe in the A'in-i Akbari. As a result, they provide valuable visual information about urban professional society in Akbar's India. The artists chosen to illustrate this unique illustrated Akhlaq-i Nasiri were not Akbar's major artists but rather painters trained by them.

A. W.

1. Abu'l-Fazl, A'in-i Akbari, trans. H. Blochmann (Calcutta, 1927), 1:110.
2. For a splendid translation of this text and an excellent introduction to its author, see G. M. Wickens, trans., The Nasirean Ethics, by Nasir al-Din Tusi (London, 1964).
3. For this calligrapher, see cat. no. 56.
4. See cat. no. 59.
5. Tulsi Kalan and Khim Karan worked on the Victoria and Albert Akbarnamah (see cat. no. 52). Khim Karan and Dhanraj provided paintings for the Chester Beatty Akbarnamah; and Tulsi Kalan and Dhanraj participated in a Khamsah of Nizami, datable to the same period.
6. Wickens, Nasirean Ethics, p. 158.
7. Kanak Singh worked on the 1595–1596 Khamsah of Nizami (British Museum Or. 12208) and the Timurnamah in the Bankipur State Library.
8. Wickens, Nasirean Ethics, p. 216.

**59 / Two Pages of a Diwan of Shahi**

India; ca. 1595

(A)  A Prince and a Hermit
     Attrib. to Miskin
     Page: H. 26.7 cm., W. 20.3 cm.
     Miniature: H. 13.3 cm., W. 9.2 cm.

(B) A Love-Maddened Man in a City Square
  Page: H. 32.4 cm., W. 22 cm.
  Miniature: H. 12.7 cm., W. 8.1 cm.

Timur's grandson, Baysunghur Mirza (d. 1433) was one of the most gifted Timurid connoisseurs and bibliophiles, and literature and the arts flourished at his court in Herat. Among the many prominent poets who enjoyed the prince's patronage was Amir Shahi (d. 1453), and his *Diwan* was popular not only in Timurid Iran but also at the Mughal court in the sixteenth and seventeenth centuries. These two miniatures originally belonged to a small, superbly finished copy of Shahi's *Diwan*, whose miniatures are all characterized by great refinement and delicacy and a grasp of atmosphere and perspective more accomplished than in earlier, larger works done under Mughal patronage.[1] Stylistically this *Diwan* clearly belongs to a group of royal manuscripts of the first rank that was produced in the imperial atelier in Lahore and that includes the 1595 *Baharistan* of Jami[2] and the 1596 *Khamsah* of Nizami.[3] For these sumptuous books Akbar's finest painters worked without the aid of assistants. By 1595 the young prince Salim had become a gifted connoisseur of painting and calligraphy, and this late sixteenth-century group of literary manuscripts, emphasizing high finish and small size, very likely reflects his influence on Akbar's atelier.

The first miniature illustrated here, attributable to the major artist Miskin,[4] takes up a familiar theme. From the nearby city in the upper left a royal hunting party—fourteen attendants and a mustached prince—has come, initially searching for game but now stopping at the cave of a hermit, solitary except for his parrot. The verse reads: "I am the sacred parrot, imprisoned in a cage. / Where is the mirror of your face, that I may begin to talk?"[5] While his companions stand politely nearby, the prince, who resembles Akbar's son Salim and may well be a portrait of him, sits on an elegant carpet and converses with the hermit. The caged parrot is between them, and in the rocks above the hermit's head can be seen the forms of two animals and a human face. Directly to the left of the hermit's face is another bearded visage, peering out of stone at the prince.

The painter of the second miniature is so far unidentified, but the illustrative process is the same as in catalogue number 59(A): a single incident from one verse of a poem in the *Diwan* of Shahi has been amplified into an entire scene.[6] A love-maddened man holding round objects in both hands rages in a city square and drives people away from him toward the left. Perplexed men stand in a group at upper right, watching the tumult, and in the center several women peer from the shelter of a doorway. The perspective is strikingly uneven: the angry man and the figures in the

**59A** / A prince and a hermit

**59B** / A love-maddened man in a city square

upper right are far larger than all the others, and the city's buildings and walls are dwarfed in comparison with the human scale.

The text of the *Diwan* appears to have been copied by 'Abd al-Rahim al-Haravi 'Anbarin Qalam, the most important calligrapher in the Mughal atelier at that time.[7]

A. W.

1. For two other miniatures from this manuscript, see Stuart C. Welch, *The Art of Mughal India* (New York, 1963), nos. 5a and 5b. All of the miniatures have been remounted with unattractive nineteenth-century French borders, presumably supplied for this purpose by the dealer who separated the illustrations from the manuscript.

2. In the Bodleian Library, Oxford.

3. Formerly in the Dyson-Perrins Collection and now in the British Museum.

4. Mentioned by Abu'l-Fazl in the *A'in-i Akbari*, trans. H. Blochmann, 2nd ed. (Calcutta, 1907), 1:114. The painter was responsible for many miniatures in Akbar-period manuscripts. Other masters who contributed to the *Diwan* of Shahi were Basawan and Kesu Das.

5. Translated by Annemarie Schimmel, who has also pointed out that Shahi himself had been a calligrapher at the court of Prince Baysunghur in Herat. His *Diwan* was one of the most widely calligraphed texts in the late fifteenth and the sixteenth century.

6. For this observation I am indebted to Dr. Annemarie Schimmel. The same process can be seen in a *Diwan* of Anvari in the Fogg Art Museum (Gift of John Goelet), Cambridge, Mass. It belongs to the group of small, highly refined manuscripts produced in the latter part of Akbar's reign (see Annemarie Schimmel and Stuart C. Welch, *A Pocketbook for Akbar, A Diwan of Anvari Dated 1588* [New York, forthcoming]).

7. See cat. no. 56 for a discussion of this master.

PUBLISHED: (A) Stuart C. Welch "Mughal and Deccani Miniature Paintings from a Private Collection," *Ars Orientalis* 5 (1963), pp. 221–33, fig. 5. In this article, the attribution to Miskin is argued at length.

## 60 / Salim and the Captured Cheetah

By Aqa Riza
India; ca. 1602
Page: H. 38.8 cm., W. 27.4 cm.
Miniature: H. 31.1 cm., W. 19.4 cm.

*Nim qalam* (half-pen) drawings are frequent in Mughal art of the late Akbar and early Jahangir periods, and their partial painting is used to excellent effect here. The startling blue of Prince Salim's outer garment, tied loosely at his waist, draws immediate attention to Akbar's son: it is a nice courtier's touch by the painter in the prince's employ. The gold of his other garments, and his white turban, serve the same function. Fainter colors tint the clothing of lesser persons. Dark green tree leaves and the gold, blue, and white sky are the other principal areas of color.

Near the center of the enclosure the prince kneels and holds the cheetah's head as it is lifted onto a heavy cloth for transport to the cage that appears just below it in the picture; from the lower left comes a bullock cart

to take the caged cheetah back to the city of Allahabad in the upper left.[1] On the two small rocks just above the cart is the inscription: "Aqa Riza, the servant of Shah Salim."

Akbar's eldest son, Salim (b. 1569), was increasingly at odds with his father in the last decade of Akbar's rule, and in 1599–1600 (A.H. 1008) he rebelled, declared himself emperor in the city of Allahabad, and set up his own court. Though father and son were later reconciled and Salim succeeded to the Mughal throne in 1605 under the regnal name of Jahangir, the feud was a prelude to the ferocious internecine warfare that dangerously weakened the Mughal state in the seventeenth century. The ambitious prince is shown here at the age of thirty or thirty-one, in one of the many incidents recorded in his *Memoirs* that reveal his fascination with animals and with hunting.

Speaking in his *Memoirs* about his favorite painter, Abu'l-Hasan,[2] Jahangir refers briefly and somewhat disparagingly to that artist's father, Aqa Riza: "His father, Aqa Riza, of Herat, at the time when I was prince, joined my service. There is, however, no comparison between his work and that of his father."[3] Although not to be identified with Shah 'Abbas's court artist of the same name, Jahangir's Aqa Riza came from a similar stylistic background,[4] and his earliest datable works[5] establish his artistic affinity with Iranian court painting of the 1570s and 1580s (see cat. no. 30). The emperor Akbar had little taste for Safavid painting, as Abu'l-Fazl's remarks on the development of the painter 'Abd al-Samad indicate (see cat. no. 55), but the heir-apparent was initially much more open to the qualities of a master like Aqa Riza. It is thus probable that Aqa Riza entered the prince's service soon after he came from Iran, and he accompanied Salim to Allahabad, where he was the chief painter in the rebellious son's atelier.

Aqa Riza had two sons who surpassed him as painters, Abu'l-Hasan (b. 1588–1589) and 'Abid, likely born somewhat later.[6] Presumably both were trained by their father, although Jahangir gives himself much of the credit for Abu'l-Hasan's eminence.[7] Neither son adopted the father's Iranianizing mode, which Jahangir favored in Allahabad and then ignored after his accession to power (and control over the full imperial atelier) in 1605. But that short-lived style is readily apparent in this drawing: most of the figures show that lack of volume which is one of the characteristics of Safavid painting, and the occasional very bright pigments recall Iranian usage. But some details—like the bullocks, the tree and the monkeys in it, the distant city—are closer to the main currents of Mughal painting, and it has been argued in conversation by Stuart C. Welch that Aqa Riza was assisted in this drawing by his gifted son Abu'l-Hasan, who would have been at least eleven years old at this time (see cat. no. 61 for a drawing attributed to the young Abu'l-Hasan). Aqa Riza's extant oeuvre is small, and this drawing numbers among the very few works from the period when he was directly under Prince Salim's patronage in Allahabad. Further, it assists us in understanding the evolution of the future emperor Jahangir's taste, and it presents us with what may be the earliest known work of Abu'l-Hasan.[8]

A. W.

1. Akbar had developed the ancient and strategically located city of Allahabad into a major military center after 1574; five years later he established the city as capital of Allahabad Province and began a large fort there. It is presumably this architectural complex that we see in the upper left.

2. See the following entries for further discussion of Abu'l-Hasan: nos. 61, 68, 69, 71. Another recent examination is in Milo C. Beach, *The Grand Mogul* (Williamstown, Mass., 1978), pp. 86–92.

3. *Tuzuk-i Jahangiri,* trans A. Rogers and ed. H. Beveridge (London, 1909–1914), 2:20.

4. For Aqa Riza Jahangiri, see Beach, *Grand Mogul,* pp. 92–93.

5. See Laurence Binyon, J. V. S. Wilkinson, and Basil Gray, *Persian Miniature Painting* (London, 1933), pl. CIV, no. 236. In 1599–1600 (A.H. 1008) Aqa Riza also supplied illuminated margins for one of the most important Mughal albums, and the figures in these margins are closely related stylistically to those in this drawing. (See Yedda A. Godard, "Les Marges du Marakka Gulshan," *Athar-i Iran,* vol. 1, fasc. 1 [1936], pp. 11–36.)

6. For 'Abid, see Beach, *Grand Mogul,* p. 85.

7. *Tuzuk-i Jahangiri,* p. 20.

8. The drawing has been remounted; its present borders are of considerably later date. On the reverse is an eighteenth-century design of a tree with pink blossoms and four perched birds.

## 61 / Dalliance in the Country

Attrib. to Abu'l-Hasan

India; ca. 1601

Page: H. 38.8 cm., W. 28.5 cm.

Miniature: H. 20.5 cm., W. 12.6 cm.

On the raised porch of a square pavilion sit a young man and a young woman, both elegantly dressed. His trousers are tinted rose, as is her long veil, and there are touches of the same color in the flowers and in the fence that encloses the building. A distant landscape, complete with city, forest, and tiny shrine, adds a Mughal cliché to the romantic scene, but it is almost overwhelmed by the bursting foliage of a great tree. Just inside the fence are two bird cages and three stacked bowls, all powerfully but rather awkwardly rendered, and the little boy in the lower center seems visually somewhat related to similar children in Safavid painting. The old woman in the lower left is, however, based on acute observation and is a brilliant, if somewhat rough, study. Clearly this drawing, with its combination of repeated formulae and innovation, is not the work of a long-established master but instead of a greatly talented youthful draftsman just emerging from his apprenticeship and displaying a predictable mixture of dependence and independence.

Certain elements hint at both training and identity. The tree's explosive vigor recalls the tree in Aqa Riza's drawing of Prince Salim and the cheetah (cat. no. 60), and the face of the attentive young man is almost identical

**61** /

with that of the attendant with the fly whisk standing behind Salim. Since this youth's face is also comparable with Abu'l-Hasan's first dated work, a 1600–1601 drawing of St. John after Dürer,[1] an attribution of this work to Abu'l-Hasan seems convincing.

Further evidence of the precocious Abu'l-Hasan is apparent if we compare this drawing with one of Mughal art's more puzzling masterpieces, the famed *Bullock Cart* in the Sah Collection, Banaras, a brilliant miniature in which Abu'l-Hasan's signature is worked into the design of the cart itself.[2] In addition, this miniature contains precisely the same moon-shaped faces seen in the present drawing; and as in the present drawing, the overall spirit is more rugged, even raw, than one would have expected in a great painting of the early seventeenth century. Coincidentally, the bullocks and cart in the Banaras picture can be seen as more articulately refined versions of the same passages in catalogue number 60, passages which we assign unhesitatingly to the very young Abu'l-Hasan rather than to his far less gifted but at that time more accomplished father. *Dalliance in the Country,* therefore, can be regarded as Abu'l-Hasan's earliest extant work, datable to about 1601.[3] *Salim and the Captured Cheetah,* on which the boy collaborated with his father, should be dated slightly later, and the Banaras *Bullock Cart* to about 1603.

During the early years of the seventeenth century, when father and son worked in the studios of the art-loving Prince Salim at Allahabad, Abu'l-Hasan's youthful energy seems to have drawn him to the dynamic style associated with the *Hamzanamah* as well as to European prints and his father's calligraphically elegant, markedly Iranian manner. His genius, however, was already evident; and one finds justification in his juvenilia for the high regard in which he was held by his judicious patron.

S. C. W. and A. W.

1. See Basil Gray, K. de B. Codrington, and John Irwin, *The Arts of India and Pakistan* (exhib. cat.; London: Royal Academy of Arts, 1947–1948), fig. 665.
2. Reproduced in N. C. Mehta, *Studies in Indian Painting* (Bombay, 1926), facing p. 64.
3. This drawing is mounted now as an album page with much later borders. The reverse is blank. On the obverse, about three centimeters above the drawing, is written in Persian in a very rough hand, "The work of Master Black Pen (draftsman)." It is not a signature and was presumably added when the drawing was mounted in the album.

## 62 / An Elephant of Many Parts

India; ca. 1600
Page: H. 39 cm., W. 25 cm.
Miniature: H. 13.4 cm., W. 20 cm.

There is a compelling tradition of composite animals in Islamic art, and this Mughal painting is one of its most complex, vital, and impressive

**62** / Reverse

embodiments.[1] Walking in front of the elephant and looking back at the royal rider is a guide, painted white except for his pink scarf: his color presumably is associated with the picture's wider meaning. The brilliantly colored elephant and rider are in bright contrast to the *nim qalam* background. Blowing behind the king's gold crown are flames; his belt is a living snake; and his garment, composed of animal bodies, merges with the composite animals forming the elephant: the rider's legs become part of his mount. From the elephant's neck and belly hang two bells, the first a golden monkey head, the second a golden lion head. The body of the elephant itself partakes of dozens of forms that fall into four groups: (1) predators—lions, tigers, and mythological orange *kylins,* almost all with some creature in their jaws; (2) prey—cows, deer, and other quadrupeds; (3) birds—neither hunters nor hunted, crammed into the spaces between the other creatures or forming specific elephant parts, like the fat quail that compose the feet or the duck that forms the lower jaw; (4) men—also onlookers rather than actors, with the arms of the foremost man turning into the elephant's tusks, which end in human hands holding feathers. There are puzzles too in this bewildering pachyderm world: the elephant has no visible ear or eye, and a snake drips from the elephant's trunk, although elephants and snakes are natural enemies. And not all is serious: a spotted cow, pressed up against an elephant's head and attacked by a lion, lets out a bellow of complaint.

It is a complex creation but one that gives the sense not of a unique vision but rather of a traditional image rendered with uncommon vitality. The painter is not known, and the picture's meaning is neither obvious nor defined in textual sources. One can suggest that the white guide is a Sufi, leading the royal rider who is very much in control of this human and animal diversity—a metaphor of the Mughals, who aspired to Solomon-like kingship under divine auspices. Thus, like catalogue number 63, the image is a mixture of the worldly and otherworldly, of the possible and impossible. That is perhaps why the many birds—traditional symbols of the human soul in Sufi thought and imagery—are both in the midst of it and beyond it and are, in fact, the feet lifting the immense weight of the world.

A narrow blue-green border with gold arabesques was added around the miniature at a later date. The margins resemble those of catalogue number 56—birds, deer, gazelles, and a hunting cheetah—and are the work of the same illuminator, a follower of the Master of the Borders. They, like the border, date to about 1640.

The Master of the Borders was responsible for the stately, elegant floral margins of the reverse, which also recall those of catalogue number 56. They enclose a fine calligraphy, written diagonally in Persian and Arabic:

May God honor his face.
From the Sayings of the Leader of the Believers,
    Hazrat 'Ali:
Since I knew God, I never rendered thanks to nor
    made any complaints about one of His creatures,
Because all that came to me, I saw from Him.
The poor sinner 'Abdullah al-Husayni, may
    God forgive his sins and hide his faults.[2]

'Abdullah al-Husayni is known as a prominent calligrapher at the court of
Shah Jahan, where he was granted the honorary appellation (*khitab*) Mish-
kin Qalam, or Musk Pen.[3] This work, in *ta'liq* style, probably dates to about
1640–1645, the years when the album was presumably assembled. Obverse
and reverse margins were obviously once part of the same album and may
have been side by side.

A. W.

1. For several examples of composite animals of various sorts, see Anthony Welch, *Shah
'Abbas and the Arts of Isfahan* (New York, 1973), no. 59; idem, *Calligraphy in the Arts of the Muslim
World* (Austin and London, 1979), no. 77; Stuart C. Welch, *Indian Drawings and Painted Sketches*
(New York, 1976), no. 11. The latter image is also a composite elephant and also rendered
close to 1600 by a Mughal master; this elephant, however, is led, ridden, and followed by *divs*
(demons), implying that the whole world is controlled by the preternatural. As the author
points out, such composite creatures ultimately derive from ancient and culturally diverse
sources.

2. Translation by Annemarie Schimmel.

3. Mehdi Bayani, *Khushnevisan* [Calligraphers] (Tehran, 1966), 2:354–55. The latest known
work by his hand is dated to 1652–1653 (A.H. 1063) and is in the Bibliothèque Nationale, Paris.

## 63 / King Solomon's Court
Attrib. to Madhu Khanahzad
India; ca. 1600
Page: H. 34.5 cm., W. 22.8 cm.
Miniature: H. 27.4 cm., W. 15.5 cm.

In sympathy [he was like] Jacob,
In comeliness [like] Joseph,
In fortitude [like] John,
In sovereignty [like] Solomon.

These laudatory similes are written in a graceful *nasta'liq* in the two
panels near the top of the painting: the use of Old and New Testament
figures as exemplars of virtue is common in Islamic literatures. Like the
Mughal emperor Akbar,[1] King Sulayman (Solomon) in *darbar* (court recep-

tion) sits on a throne, hexagonal like the orange canopy shading him and the carpets and platform beneath. Birds fill the cloud-streaked blue sky or perch in trees, while the ruler hears of the approach of the Queen of Sheba from a hoopoe perched to his left on the throne. Angels stand around him; *jinn* (genies), brought firmly under Sulayman's control, either serve or stand in readiness. A page boy behind the king's right shoulder holds a fly whisk; the only other human present is his *vazir*, seated on the platform of the throne. Animals too accept the great king's sovereignty. They gather, mostly in pairs (presumably an indication of fecundity), obediently at the bottom of the miniature. With a single exception, all of the animals are indigenous to India; only the *simurgh*—a mythical bird in the upper right— is not, but its presence so pervades the literary and mystical traditions of Islam that it is quite at home here.[2]

To Muslims, Sulayman was the perfect image of the ideal king. He enjoyed the closest divine support and was endowed with superb gifts— including the knowledge of all languages, human and animal—that gave him remarkable understanding of other living things. Presiding over great heterogeneity, he created and preserved harmony, and his control over natural forces, like the wind, and supernatural beings, like the *jinn*, gave him unparalleled authority.[3] The Ottoman sultans found the Sulayman image appealing, and so did the Mughals: both empires were extremely diverse in population, faiths, and languages, and the autocratic ruler was the central element binding society together. This picture, painted for Akbar in the latter part of his reign, when he had created the administrative structures that would preserve the Mughal state for the next century, is an ideal image of Mughal kingship.

Attributed to the hand of Madhu Khanahzad, one of Akbar's leading painters,[4] this miniature may have once belonged to a *Diwan* of Hafiz.[5]

A. W.

1. Scenes similar in composition are found in the Victoria and Albert Museum's *Akbar-namah*, as well as in other Mughal historical manuscripts.

2. The *simurgh* in Iranian mystical poetry is often a symbol of the divine essence. For a brief discussion, see Anthony Welch, *Calligraphy in the Arts of the Muslim World* (Austin and London, 1979), no. 83.

3. For a discussion of Sulayman, see Welch, *Calligraphy*, nos. 30 and 82. For references to Sulayman in the Qur'an, see 21:78–82, 27:15–44, 34:12–14, 38:30–40.

4. See Stuart C. Welch, "Early Mughal Miniature Paintings from Two Private Collections," *Ars Orientalis* 3 (1959):139–40 and fig. 11.

5. See idem, "Miniatures from a Manuscript of the *Diwan* of Hafiz," *Marg* 11 (June 1958):3.

PUBLISHED: René Grousset, *The Civilisations of the East: India* (London, 1932), fig. 218; J. Strzygowski, *Asiatische Miniaturmalerei* (Vienna, 1933), pl. 80, fig. 216; Welch, "Early Mughal Miniature Paintings," no. 8 and fig. 11; Stuart C. Welch and Milo C. Beach, *Gods, Thrones and Peacocks* (New York, 1965), no. 6.

**64** / A Manuscript of the *Kulliyat* of Sa'di
India; ca. 1604
H. 42.5 cm., W. 27.5 cm.

The *Bustan* (*Garden*) and *Gulistan* (*Rose Garden*) of the thirteenth-century Iranian poet Sa'di were among the most popular and frequently illustrated books in the Islamic world, particularly in Mughal India, where sumptuous copies were made for both Akbar and Jahangir.[1] Less often, Sa'di's oeuvre would be presented in a *Kulliyat* (Collected Works) that included not only the *Bustan* and *Gulistan* but also his many other verse and prose compositions in Arabic and Persian.[2] Such a book was a large undertaking, and this manuscript is the only extant lavishly produced imperial Mughal *Kulliyat*. Its 195 leaves are larger than those in most royal books of the period; of the 390 pages, 57 are blank but have the same gold margins as the rest of the manuscript. Since the text is complete, these pages were presumably intended for additional illuminations or illustrations.[3] On folio 1a is the seal of Shah Jahan, an indication that the book was a treasured royal possession. The colophon on folio 195b identifies the book and the scribe but mentions no date, site, or patron and lists none of the several painters and illuminators who provided the twenty-three miniatures and five illuminated title pages. The calligrapher, 'Abd al-Rahim al-Haravi, enjoyed the highest reputation and favor under Akbar and Jahangir, who gave him the honorific 'Anbarin Qalam (Amber Pen).[4]

Although undated, the *Kulliyat* undoubtedly was produced about 1604 and belongs to a key group of manuscripts marking the aesthetic transition between the patronage of the two emperors.[5] In 1604 Akbar's studio completed the first half of a large *Akbarnamah* measuring 42.1 by 27.7 centimeters; the second half was almost certainly finished in the first year of Jahangir's reign.[6] The text was written by Muhammad Husayn al-Kashmiri, whom Akbar called Zarin Qalam (Golden Pen), as highly esteemed a scribe as 'Abd al-Rahim al-Haravi.[7] Its illustrations delineate this transitional period: masters like Basawan and Kesu the Elder, who had been instrumental in developing Mughal painting under Akbar, are absent; others, like Farrukh Chela, Miskin, and Dharm Das, were nearing the end of long, distinguished careers; and younger artists—among them Balchand, Daulat, Dhanraj, and Govardhan, all closely associated with Jahangir—contributed to the second volume, which was probably begun after the future king returned to Agra in 1604 at the end of his five-year rebellion.

Reflecting Jahangir's taste even more fully is the *Anvar-i Suhayli* in the British Museum, dated to 1604–1610.[8] Two of its paintings, both dated to 1604, are by Aqa Riza Jahangiri,[9] the Iranian master who flourished under Jahangir's patronage from 1599 to 1605, when the young emperor inherited

**64** / folio 28b: Dara and the herdsman

**64** / folio 65b: The Prince of Khotan, the ascetic, and the hungry man

**64** / folio 78b: Saʿdi and the idol of Somnath

**64** / folio 91a: Saʿdi and his patron Abu Bakr ibn Saʿd ibn Zangi

the royal atelier and apparently soon lost interest in Aqa Riza's style. It was in that first year of the new reign that a second Sa'di manuscript was created, a 1605–1606 *Bustan*, its colophon recording that it was completed in Agra by 'Abd al-Rahim al-Haravi 'Anbarin Qalam.[10] Two of its twenty-two illustrations are clearly the work of Aqa Riza Jahangiri,[11] and other of its miniatures have been attributed to Abu'l-Hasan, Govardhan, Mirza Ghulam, and Sur Das Gujarati.[12]

Comparison with these three manuscripts reliably establishes the contemporaneity of this *Kulliyat*. In size and stylistic range it is almost identical with the *Akbarnamah* of about 1604, written by Muhammad Husayn, the long-time colleague of 'Abd al-Rahim. The two calligraphers were thus working at the same time on separate projects of similar importance and magnitude. Completing the *Kulliyat* in the first year of Jahangir's reign, 'Abd al-Rahim was immediately assigned the second Sa'di project, the 1605–1606 *Bustan*, and many of the *Kulliyat* painters went with him to the new task, a scaled-down and more portable version of part of the *Kulliyat*. The *Anvar-i Suhayli* of 1604–1610 also spans these years, and Aqa Riza Jahangiri, who apparently disappears from the scene in 1605–1606, provided two paintings for it, as he did for the *Bustan*.

Like the contemporary *Akbarnamah*, the *Kulliyat* of circa 1604 contains paintings by Akbari and Jahangiri masters. In the lower margins of folios 78b (illustrated) and 89b are ascriptions in red ink to Dharm Das and Hiranand respectively; the latter probably also painted folios 58a and 160a.[13] Both came from Akbar's long-established atelier, as did Farrukh Chela, who must also have contributed to the manuscript. Folio 91a (illustrated), however, is surely the work of Aqa Riza Jahangiri, and it is probable that other artists—like Abu'l-Hasan, Govardhan, Mirza Ghulam, Daulat, and Sur Das Gujarati, who took part in the illustration of the 1605–1606 *Bustan*—were actively involved in the great *Kulliyat*.[14]

Folio 28b (illustrated) is unsigned and illustrates one of the initial tales of the *Bustan*. Separated from his hunting party, the emperor Dara prepares to defend himself against an approaching herdsman whom he takes to be an enemy. Identifying himself as Dara's own herdsman, the man gently but pointedly upbraids the emperor:

> It's neither laudable provision nor good
>     judgment
> When the emperor knows not enemy from friend!
> It is in high station a condition of living
> That you should know who each inferior is.[15]

The same artist was also responsible for folio 41b.

Folio 65b (illustrated) is a tour de force illustrating two of the *Bustan's* moral stories. The first four couplets describe the Prince of Khotan's gift of a silk scarf to an ascetic who did not value worldly treasures,[16] and the remaining five couplets begin the anecdote of the hungry man who was driven away from a feast.[17] The upper portion of the illustration appears to show the prince of Khotan; the lower section illustrates the feast from which the poor man is being repelled in the lower right.[18]

Dharm Das illustrates one of the most celebrated stories in the *Bustan* on folio 78b. At one point in his extensive travels Sa'di stopped at the great temple of Somnath in India, where he engaged in religious discussion with Brahmin priests. To his explication and praise of Islam they responded by demonstrating that the temple's idol gestured in response to their prayers. Initially confounded, Sa'di inspected the statue at night and discovered a mechanical device that operated the image's arms. And on the following day he vindicated his own position by confronting the priests with their trickery.[19]

Aqa Riza's single contribution to the *Kulliyat* is folio 91a, a picture that should probably be considered as illustrating both the *Bustan* and the *Gulistan*, for it depicts the pious Sa'di with his prayer beads, book, pen, and paper, seated with Abu Bakr ibn Sa'd ibn Zangi, the patron who is eulogized at the beginning of both the *Bustan* and the *Gulistan*. Through a skillful combination of tribute and alliance, this ruler of southern Iran had protected Sa'di's beloved city of Shiraz from the Mongol incursions of the mid-thirteenth century; he had also supported the poet, as the tray of gold coins between them indicates. Though not a Mongol, Abu Bakr wears Mongol headgear that identifies him as an ally of the invaders.

The iconography of *Bustan* illustration was well developed: fifteen of the *Kulliyat's* miniatures illustrate it. Four miniatures are devoted to the *Gulistan*, and four more paintings illustrate the remainder of the *Kulliyat*.

A. W.

1. Among them are the following: 1581 *Gulistan* (Royal Asiatic Society, London); ca. 1595–1600 *Gulistan* (dispersed); 1605–1606 *Bustan* (private collection); ca. 1610–1615 *Gulistan* (dispersed); ca. 1620 *Bustan* (Collection of Philip Hofer).

2. The *Kulliyat* was sometimes referred to as the *Sa'dinamah* [Book of Sa'di], the term used in this manuscript's colophon.

3. The manuscript is paginated as follows: fols. 1b–19b, preface; 21b–89b, *Bustan*; 91b–130a, *Gulistan*; 132b–195a, Sa'di's remaining shorter works.

4. For 'Abd al-Rahim al-Haravi 'Anbarin Qalam, see cat. no. 56.

5. For an analysis of this group of manuscripts and this period, see Milo C. Beach, *The Grand Mogul* (Williamstown, Mass., 1978), pp. 23–25, 41–43, and passim; idem, *The Imperial Image, Paintings for the Mughal Court* (Washington, D.C., 1981), pp. 24–26, 102–23, and passim.

6. The first portion, probably begun in 1602 and completed in 1604, is in the British Library; the second part, undated but almost certainly completed early in Jahangir's reign, is in the Chester Beatty Library in Dublin. Many illustrations are separated and dispersed from both sections. For further discussion and bibliography, see Beach, *Imperial Image*, pp. 102–23. For a page from the first *Akbarnamah*, produced about 1590 for Akbar, see cat. no. 52.

7. For Muhammad Husayn Zarin Qalam, see cat. no. 57.

8. See J. V. S. Wilkinson, *The Lights of Canopus* (London, 1929).

9. For Aqa Riza, see cat. nos. 60, 61.

10. The *Bustan* is in private possession. I am most grateful to its owner for allowing me to study it, for giving me a set of slides of its illustrations, and for sharing with me many thoughtful insights about the book. The manuscript is discussed at length in Beach, *Grand Mogul;* idem, *Imperial Image;* Stuart C. Welch, *The Art of Mughal India* (New York, 1963), nos. 23, 24; and Ivan Stchoukine, "Un Bustan de Sa'di illustré par des artistes Moghols," *Revue des arts asiatiques* 11 (1937):68–74.

11. One is reproduced in Stuart C. Welch, *The Art of Mughal India*, no. 24.

12. By Beach, *Imperial Image*, pp. 164, 167, 194, 228.

13. Attribution by Beach, *Imperial Image*, p. 116.

14. The dispersed *Gulistan* of ca. 1610–1615 contains paintings by many of the same masters and may have been intended as a companion volume to the 1605–1606 *Bustan*. See Beach, *Grand Mogul*, pp. 66–70.

15. G. M. Wickens, trans., *Morals Pointed and Tales Adorned: The Bustan of Sa'di* (Toronto and Buffalo, 1974), p. 30. Subsequent *Bustan* references are to Wickens's fine translation.

16. Ibid., p. 171.

17. Ibid.

18. This same master of *nim qalam* also did folio 125a.

19. Wickens, *Bustan*, p. 214.

PUBLISHED: Ralph H. Pinder-Wilson, *Paintings from the Muslim Courts of India* (London, 1976), no. 72; Beach, *Grand Mogul*, pp. 25, 66, 69, 175, 176; and idem, *Imperial Image*, pp. 107, 111, 115–16, 228.

## 65 / A Noble Hunt

Attrib. to Muhammad 'Ali
India; ca. 1610–1615
Page: H. 36.6 cm., W. 26 cm.
Miniature: H. 19.2 cm., W. 16.3 cm.

It is the most elegant of hunts, though a hunt by inference only, since we see no prey. The horse and rider are in flawless form, their demeanor exemplifying well-trained grace as they poise (and pose) in a dance of confident assurance in their own perfection. Wearing an orange robe and golden turban, the prince has picked an arrow from his quiver as his stallion—his legs and tail half-hennaed—prepares to gallop: both seem to have just spotted the game. The horse's gold saddle and saddlecloth, anklets, and other accoutrements are rich with flowers, as sumptuous as any Mughal illuminated page.[1] Either the painter or an assistant was a master of illumination.

The foreground, over which the horse's hooves hover, is filled with flowers, as precisely rendered as those in an illuminated border. Above the distant gray background rises a purple-streaked gold sky. Four illuminated panels, two above and two below the miniature, contain verses from a less-than-impressive poem; both script and background date to about three decades later than the picture.

**65** / (also in color)

So too does the floral margin, attributable, like several other decorated margins in this exhibition, to the unidentified Master of the Borders.[2] Single large flowering plants are placed in delicate oblong frames, and smaller flowers of varied colors fill the spaces between and around them. The jewel-like setting and the placement of the flowers is reminiscent of the inlaid stonework of the Taj Mahal, under construction at this time, and the Master of the Borders may well have been responsible for some of those designs. The borders are from a great album made for Shah Jahan, later broken up, and presumably added here as an elegant setting by the art dealer Demotte.

Though a Mughal painting of a Mughal prince, the miniature shows distinct signs—particularly in the choice and juxtaposition of colors, in the floral foreground, and in a figural grace and elegance closely reminiscent of Safavid Iranian painting—of Deccani influence from the central Indian Muslim courts, where painting owed much to Persian prototypes. Very close similarities to three paintings ascribed to the master Muhammad ʿAli allow a virtually certain attribution of this miniature to the same artist. Muhammad ʿAli, like his contemporary Farrukh Beg,[3] must have spent some time at one of the Deccani courts before joining Jahangir's atelier, where he was surely one of the preeminent figures.[4]

A. W.

1. See Anthony Welch, *Calligraphy in the Arts of the Muslim World* (Austin and London, 1979), no. 85, and Milo C. Beach, *The Grand Mogul* (Williamstown, Mass., 1978), no. 21, for two examples of Mughal illuminations dating to the reign of Shah Jahan.

2. See cat. nos. 56, 57, 62, 73, as well as a portrait of Shah Jahan on the Peacock Throne in Basil W. Robinson et al., *Persian and Mughal Art* (London, 1976), fig. 95. Cat. no. 72 offers a more extensive discussion of this master.

3. For Farrukh Beg, see Robert Skelton, "The Mughal Artist Farrokh Beg," *Ars Orientalis* 2 (1957):393–411. The painter served in Bijapur between ca. 1600 and 1610.

4. Two miniatures bear attributions to Muhammad ʿAli: *Reading Youth with Falcon*, Freer Gallery of Art, Washington, D.C., no. 53.93 (see Richard Ettinghausen, *Paintings of the Sultans and Emperors of India* [New Delhi, 1961], pl. 9); and *Poet in a Garden*, Museum of Fine Arts, Boston (see Skelton, "Farrokh Beg," fig. 17; Douglas Barrett and Basil Gray, *Painting of India* [Lausanne, 1963; reprint ed., New York, 1978], p. 125; and Stuart C. Welch, *Imperial Mughal Painting* [New York, 1978], pl. 20). There seems no reason to doubt their attributions. A third work—a painting of a standing girl—is also inscribed with what appears to be the signature of the artist, "Muhammad ʿAli Jahangir Shahi," indicating that he was in the emperor's employ. The stylistic resemblance between this painting and *A Noble Hunt* is so close that the attribution of the latter to Muhammad ʿAli working in Jahangir's employ is beyond question (see Sotheby's catalogue, London, 4 February 1972, lot 111; and Edwin Binney, 3rd, *Indian Miniature Painting from the Collection of Edwin Binney, 3rd: The Mughal and Deccani Schools* [Portland, Ore., 1973], no. 123).

PUBLISHED: Ivan Stchoukine, "Portraits moghols, IV: La Collection du Baron Maurice de Rothschild," *Revue des arts asiatiques* 9 (1935):190–208, pl. 69, and fig. 6; Skelton, "Farrokh Beg," fig. 9.

## 66 / Jahangir's Lion Hunt

By Farrukh-i Khurd-i Chela
India; ca. 1610
Page: H. 28.4 cm., W. 21.8 cm.
Miniature: H. 26.8 cm., W. 20 cm.

This painting is not circumspect. The emperor, at center stage, deals a mortal blow to the lionness mauling one of his officers, who is desperately trying to defend himself with his *katar* (dagger). The picture's middle ground is all turmoil: the unnamed officer's horse dashes away to the left, while Jahangir's son, Prince Parviz, rushes in from the right and delivers another killing stroke. Suhrab Khan, seated behind Jahangir on the elephant, gesticulates wildly to keep his balance. In the upper right a lion chases four hunters up a tree, while four others keep cover in the lower right. In comparison, the miniature's upper and lower left are areas of calm.

For well over two millennia in the ancient Near East and the Islamic world, the royal hunt had been used to demonstrate a monarch's power and right to rule. Yet despite its iconographic antiquity, this scene seems fresh and vital. It records a real event, one in which Jahangir took great pride, and the painter renders it like a skilled courtier, focusing attention on the emperor's total concentration, which accomplishes the lion's death as surely as his spear.

*Nasta'liq* inscriptions on the reverse identify Jahangir, Parviz, and Suhrab Khan. Prince Parviz, who died in 1625 at the age of thirty-eight, appears to be in his early twenties here, and the emperor, born in 1569, seems about forty. The event and this pictorial record of it must date, therefore, to about 1610.

A second inscription, in what may be Jahangir's own hand, identifies the painter as Farrukh-i Khurd-i Chela, of whom works dating from about 1580 to about 1620 are known.[1]

A. W.

1. The artist is also known as Farrukh Beg and Farrukh Chela. For his career, see Robert Skelton, "The Mughal Artist Farrokh Beg," *Ars Orientalis* 2 (1957):393–411 (according to this biography, the artist would have been about sixty-four years old in 1610); and Anand Krishna, "A Study of the Akbari Artist—Farrukh Chela," in *Chhavi: Golden Jubilee Volume*, 1971, pp. 353–73. There are three other renderings of this subject: (*a*) in the collection of Prince Sadruddin Aga Khan and published in T. Falk et al., *Indian Painting* (London, 1978). This version has only minor differences, including slightly paler tone, from the painting shown here; an English inscription on the reverse correctly attributes it to Farrukh Chela; (*b*) in the Bodleian Library, Oxford, Ms. Douce Or. a.L, f. 33r. This painting is discussed in Robert Skelton, "Two Mughal Lion Hunts," *Victoria and Albert Museum Book* (1969), pp. 33–48; (*c*) in a private collection; published in T. Falk and S. Digby, *Paintings from Mughal India* (London, 1980), no. 15.

**67** / Portrait of Shah ʿAbbas I of Iran
By Bishndas
India; ca. 1618–1620
Page: H. 34.4 cm., W. 22.3 cm.
Miniature: H. 15.8 cm., W. 8 cm.

A plain green background centers our attention on the figure wearing orange boots and a dark blue garment: all three colors are muted in tone and without embellishment. They serve, however, to set off his elaborate belt and turban and focus our attention on the man's intelligent face. The twisted belt is made of gold, blue, yellow, and white cloth with the elaborately dyed underside turned up at the right, and he thrusts his hands into it with confident nonchalance, alongside a richly jeweled knife, more Mughal than Safavid in appearance. The elegant turban billows like a white cumulus, bound with a gold- and white-striped cloth whose ends are brilliant red and gold. Cool calculation and determination are revealed in the face. Altogether, this portrait presents neither volume nor shading, and in its studied flatness stands apart from most Mughal portraiture of the period. It is a deftly balanced combination of the spare and the extravagant, all directed at presenting a penetrating, almost "psychological," study.

In the lower left in a small gold cloud is the name Bishndas, one of the leading artists at Jahangir's court. The words "Likeness of ʿAli Khan" are written in the lower right. It is a later inscription. Whoever ʿAli Khan was, he is not shown here, for the person portrayed by Bishndas is the great Safavid Shah of Iran, ʿAbbas I (r. 1587–1629).[1]

The fifth shah of his dynasty, ʿAbbas was a gifted military leader and skillful administrator, who created in seventeenth-century Iran a state that for several decades rivaled its Ottoman and Mughal neighbors. Territorial ambitions to the west were satisfied by victories against the Ottoman empire; the city of Qandahar was the focus of ʿAbbas's eastern inclinations, though it was claimed and defended by the Mughals. After an unsuccessful attempt to seize the city in 1607, ʿAbbas tried diplomacy: several Iranian embassies traveled to the Mughal court, and in 1618 Jahangir responded by dispatching a lavishly accoutred mission to Iran's capital, Isfahan. Accompanying the ambassador, Khan ʿAlam, was the painter Bishndas, whom Jahangir praised in his autobiographical *Tuzuk-i Jahangiri:*

> At the time when I sent Khan ʿAlam to Persia, I had sent with him a painter of the name of Bishan Das, who was unequalled in his age for taking likenesses, to take the portraits of the Shah and the chief men of his state, and bring them. He had drawn the likenesses of most of them, and especially had taken that of my brother the Shah exceedingly well, so that

67 /

when I showed it to any of his servants, they said it was exceedingly well drawn.[2]

Cultural ties and mutual influences between the Safavid and Mughal states were many, and it is probably due to the presence and activities of Bishndas that Shah ʿAbbas in turn ordered his favorite painter, Riza, to produce portraits of the ambassador, Khan ʿAlam.[3] Though competent records of appearance, these Safavid paintings lack the psychological insight of Bishndas's renderings. Both Akbar and Shah Jahan were patrons of portraiture, but neither appears to have shared Jahangir's faith in its power to reveal the inner spirit, character, and intentions of the person portrayed. And Jahangir was keenly interested in a correct perception of ʿAbbas, his brother-monarch who kept nibbling away at Jahangir's city of Qandahar. Bishndas's several portraits of ʿAbbas served as the basis for the celebrated "political cartoons" produced for Jahangir by Abu'l-Hasan and Bichitr, which effectively used pictorial techniques borrowed from European broadsides.[4] So pleased was Jahangir with Bishndas's performance of his commission that he rewarded him with the gift of an elephant. Politically, however, the portraits, and the insight Jahangir may have gained from them, failed of their purpose: Shah ʿAbbas attacked and captured Qandahar in 1622. The Mughals did not recover it until 1638, only to lose it to the Safavids again in 1648.

The outer margins of the page are decorated with gold animal images; these borders originally belonged to a page of the *Farhang-i Jahangiri*, a dictionary compiled on Jahangir's orders and dismembered in the late nineteenth or early twentieth century by the French art dealer Demotte in order to use its margins around less elegantly bordered miniatures. Just to the left of the blue and gold floral border is a short love poem, written at some unknown time and unrelated to the portrait of ʿAbbas or, presumably, to the *Farhang-i Jahangiri*:

> I have an idol as slender as a hair,
> And to my eyes the world has become as dark as you.[5]

A. W.

1. For Shah ʿAbbas and his patronage of the arts, see Anthony Welch, *Shah ʿAbbas and the Arts of Isfahan* (New York, 1973); and idem, *Artists for the Shah* (New Haven and London, 1976).

2. *Tuzuk-i Jahangiri*, trans. A. Rogers, ed. H. Beveridge (London, 1909–1914), 2:116–117.

3. Bishndas also painted a group portrait of the meeting of Shah ʿAbbas and Khan ʿAlam (reproduced in Milo C. Beach, *The Grand Mogul* [Williamstown, Mass., 1978], p. 109). For studies of the artistic results of the exchange of embassies, see Ernst Kühnel, "Han ʿAlam und die diplomatischen Beziehungen zwischen Gehangir und Shah ʿAbbas," *Zeitschrift der deutschen morgenländischen Gesellschaft*, vol. 96 (1942); Basil W. Robinson, "Shah ʿAbbas and the

Mughal Ambassador Khan 'Alam: The Pictorial Record," *Burlington Magazine* 827 (February 1972):58–63; and Welch, *Shah 'Abbas and the Arts of Isfahan,* pp. 123, 135.

4. See Richard Ettinghausen, *Paintings of the Sultans and Emperors of India* (New Delhi, 1961), nos. 12, 13.

5. Translation by Annemarie Schimmel.

PUBLISHED: Ivan Stchoukine, "Portraits moghols IV: La Collection du Baron Maurice de Rothschild," *Revue des arts asiatiques* 9 (1935):190–208, no. 2 (not illustrated); Beach, *Grand Mogul,* p. 111 (not illustrated).

## 68 / An Aged Pilgrim

By Abu'l-Hasan
India; ca. 1615–1620
Page: H. 36.7 cm., W. 24.5 cm.
Miniature: H. 11.6 cm., W. 6.4 cm.

Fascination with the human condition and the varieties of human appearance characterizes Jahangir's patronage, and although much of his artists' work, predictably, comprises portraits of himself, his family,[1] and the court grandees, it also includes many depictions of humbler souls. Some are shown as minor figures in a large, grander scene such as the great group portrait of Jahangir at the *jharoka* window of the Agra Fort (cat. no. 69), but others appear as sensitive single studies of persons or types by whom the emperor was fascinated. The wandering holy man here, telling his beads as he struggles toward Enlightenment, is reminiscent of the mullah or Sufi in the darkened room in Agra Fort (see cat. no. 69), but he was never part of a larger composition. He is an exotic, portrayed alone and for his own sake, like the wondrous flowers, strange animals, and wasted human beings also depicted at Jahangir's command.[2]

The holy man stoops with age and perhaps with the burden of his search, and he leans heavily on his staff, but his eyes, peering intently ahead, are keen. His sinewy body testifies to long journeys and lean diet. The black space behind him merges imperceptibly with the ground he walks on, which is defined and highlighted by a few blades of grass, some small flowers, and a luxuriant, pink-blossoming plant in the lower right. Over the right shoulder of his light blue cloak hangs the strap of his beggar's sack, and on it, faintly written, is the correct attribution, "The work of Nadir al-Zaman." Nadir al-Zaman, meaning Rarity of the World, was a title bestowed on Abu'l-Hasan by the appreciative Jahangir. This brilliant study transforms what must have been a common sight in Jahangir's India into a highly singular image of spiritual dignity. It also illustrates the phenomenal range of Abu'l-Hasan's talent and Jahangir's patronage, from formal compositions on a grand scale to highly personal,

68 /

intimate portraits like this one (see cat. nos. 60, 61, 69, and 71 for other works by Abu'l-Hasan).[3]

A. W.

1. One of the most remarkable and appealing of these family portraits is Abu'l-Hasan's portrait of an infant Mughal prince (see Stuart C. Welch, *The Art of Mughal India* [New York, 1963], pl. 31).

2. See A. K. Das, *Mughal Painting during Jahangir's Time* (Calcutta, 1978), figs. 49, 50, 56, 57, 66.

3. The borders and margins around this miniature were added by the French art dealer Demotte.

PUBLISHED: Percy Brown, *Indian Painting under the Mughals* (Oxford, 1924), pl. XVII and fig. 1; Milo C. Beach, *The Grand Mogul* (Williamstown, Mass., 1978), p. 91.

## 69 / Jahangir at the *Jharoka* Window

By Abu'l-Hasan
India; ca. 1620
Page: H. 55.5 cm., W. 35 cm.
Miniature: H. 31.2 cm., W. 20 cm.

Akbar had been the great organizer of the Mughal empire, and the structures he created were basic to its strength for the century after his death. His son Jahangir inherited an established empire, which he administered with a strong sense of duty and a personal commitment to social stability and justice. Since the Mughal emperor was central to the continuance of the state, it became customary with Jahangir for the ruler to appear each day, either at court receptions (*darbar*) or, more distantly, at a special palace window (*jharoka*). In both cases it was incumbent upon resident officials and aristocrats to assemble before the emperor according to their rank. They presented a microcosm of the diversity and order of the Mughal state.

In this painting Jahangir looks down from the *jharoka* window of the Agra Fort. His aura emphasizes his role as divinely ordained leader of the state. In two smaller windows on either side are the profiles of two princes, who do not look down but instead gaze filially at their father. Though they are not identified, it is suggested that they are Prince Shahriyar and Prince Jahandar, both born in 1605.[1] Near the red canopy at the left (later replaced by one of marble) is suspended a golden chain with golden bells: in his *Tuzuk-i Jahangiri* the emperor speaks of this Chain of Justice, which he installed so that petitioners ignored or rebuffed by royal officials could still attract imperial attention for redress of wrongs. Alas for good intentions! The Chain was guarded, and we see at the left a prospective petitioner being beaten away.

**69** / (also in color)

**69** / Detail

Ranged in front of the Agra Fort is the Mughal hierarchy, rank and power being signified by proximity to the emperor. Many of the figures are identified by inscriptions on their garments: on the raised white wall stand 'Itiqad Khan, Khan Jahan, 'Itimad al-Daulat, Abu'l-Hasan, and Sadiq Khan. They stand stiffly at attention, their faces either in profile or turned in steady obeisance toward the emperor. In the courtyard below the wall the scene is more relaxed, though here too several officials are identified: Qasim 'Ali Kunwal, Shafiqat Jilah, and Hasan Khan. Present as well are ambassadors or visitors from other lands, come to offer homage to the emperor; their presence implies the preeminence of the Mughal empire. The Iranian emissary is dressed in green and purple, with a gold turban; he stands in the group at the right, near a black African and an Abyssinian. Guards, musicians, attendants, and other officials bring the number of assembled onlookers to seventy-seven.

The composition mirrors the state. In the upper half, as if created by the emperor's proximity, all is hierarchical order, propriety, and calm. But the farther from the emperor, the more turbulent and noisy life becomes: guards drive away petitioners; musicians play fanfares announcing the imperial presence; a happy elephant trumpets its approval; men try to talk; and in the lower right one benighted individual blocks his ears while another gives a raucous whistle. Here is another, disorderly, world, controlled more by Jahangir's soldiers than by his lofty, distant, undirected gaze. In the very center of the painting is a small entrance into the raised marble wall, and within it can be seen either a mullah or a Sufi, probably a portrait of an as-yet-unidentified holy man who enjoyed Jahangir's favor. Though the inscription below the entrance has been blurred, he must be a very significant personage, for he is squarely at the center of the picture. The painting is a most impressive group portrait (the painter had obviously seen many such royal appearances and had closely studied the participants), but like many seventeenth-century group portraits in Europe, it is also a political statement. From bottom to top the picture moves from naturalism to symbolism and from real to ideal individuals.

Below the holy man's door is an inscription crediting the painting to Nadir al-Zaman (Rarity of the World), the honorific of Jahangir's favorite and most honored master, Abu'l-Hasan.[2] The artist was then at the height of his creative power and prestige, and this painting displays consummate mastery of portraiture, composition, and the political symbolism of Jahangir's state.

Originally, the painting belonged to a royal copy of Jahangir's autobiography, the *Jahangirnamah* (or *Tuzuk-i Jahangiri*),[3] with illustrations by almost all the leading artists of Jahangir's atelier. Its present margins were probably added later, when it was mounted as an album page. On the reverse is a fine calligraphy, four lines of *nasta'liq* rendering a poem by the

Iranian mystical poet ʿAyn al-Qadat Hamadani, who was executed in 1131. It is likely the work of the celebrated scribe Muhammad Husayn al-Kashmiri, dubbed Zarin Qalam by his admiring patron, Akbar.[4] The mystical love poem reads as follows:

Sometimes I call you Cypress, sometimes
  Moon,
And sometimes Muskdeer, fallen in the snare.
Now tell me, friend, which one do you prefer?
For out of jealousy, I'll hide your name!

A. W.

1. In cat. no. 70 the princes' names accompany their portraits. Prince Khurram (the future Shah Jahan) does not appear to be represented in this painting of his father at the *jharoka* window. Though it was not until 1623 that he rebelled actively against his father, he was not favored by Jahangir's powerful wife, Nur Jahan, who controlled the government. It is worth noting that the royal officials who are identified by name in this group portrait are all relatives or close associates of Nur Jahan, whose candidate for the succession was Prince Shahriyar. The eldest son, Khusrau, had rebelled in 1606 and had been partially blinded in 1607.

2. For Abu'l-Hasan, see cat. nos. 60, 61, 68, and 71, and Milo C. Beach, *The Grand Mogul* (Williamstown, Mass., 1978), pp. 86–92.

3. For a discussion of the royal copy (or copies) of the *Jahangirnamah*, see Beach, *Grand Mogul*, pp. 61–64.

4. For Muhammad Husayn, see cat. nos. 57 and 71, as well as Anthony Welch, *Calligraphy in the Arts of the Muslim World* (Austin and London, 1979), no. 76. We are grateful to Annemarie Schimmel for identifying the poet and the scribe and for translating the poem.

PUBLISHED: *Loan Exhibition of Antiquities, Coronation Durbar* (Delhi Museum of Archaeology), no. C508, pl. XXXVII; Beach, *Grand Mogul*, pp. 64, 91.

## 70 / Pictorial Genealogy of Jahangir
India; ca. 1620–1622
Page: H. 36.2 cm., W. 24.5 cm.

In the sixteenth and seventeenth centuries illustrated royal genealogies were produced in Ottoman Turkey and, less commonly, in Mughal India.[1] They reflect the considerable reliance of both dynasties on lineage to legitimate their claims to sovereignty over exceedingly heterogeneous populations. This carefully balanced pictorial representation of royal filiation ranks with the mid-sixteenth-century Mughal painting in the British Museum, *Princes of the House of Timur*, as an exposition of the Timurid connection that was so vital to the legitimacy of the Mughal house.[2] As it now exists, the painting is a brilliant pastiche, probably put together for Jahangir himself. At the top are three vertical sections of illumination: the predominantly blue left and right panels are nearly identical and are late

70 /

fifteenth-century Herat work; the broader panel in the center, with its large areas of gold, must have been produced in Qazvin about 1580. They were taken from other pages and remounted here to emphasize the basic vertical divisions of the groups of paintings below.

Directly below the central illumination is the largest roundel, containing a portrait of the reigning emperor, Jahangir, with the aura of kingship around his head and a falcon perched on his right hand. Thin gold lines link his roundel with those of four sons, the larger circles belonging to the elder sons. To the left is Parviz (1589–1626), who meets the emperor's gaze and extends his hands toward him: he is obviously the heir-apparent. To the right, appropriately looking at his father's back, is Khusrau (1587–1622) who had rebelled in 1606, been partially blinded in 1607, and never really forgiven. In the smaller filial roundel on the left is Shahriyar (1605–1628), and in the one on the right that touches Jahangir's is Jahandar (b. 1605). Three of Parviz's sons are shown near him, in smaller circles still: Keshwar Kosha, Durandash, and Azaram; at the right are Khusrau's four sons: Garshasp, Dawar Baksh, Rastakar, and Buland Akhtar.

A vertical line leads down from Jahangir. Almost certainly it once connected him with the portrait of his third and favorite son, Khurram (1592–1666), who would also have been shown with his sons. This set of images was, however, removed and replaced with the horizontal panel, an earlier genealogy that shows in its largest circle Miran Shah, Timur's third son, from whom the Mughals themselves were descended. Radiating from him are his six sons and three grandsons.[3] This large panel bears the name of Dhanraj, not one of the Akbar's most gifted painters but a prolific illustrator of some of the emperor's many historical manuscripts.

Khusrau died in 1622, so the central portion of the page must have been completed before that date. In 1623 Khurram rebelled, and his grievously disappointed father would then have had his portrait removed from the family genealogy. Thus the picture was probably completed between 1620 and 1622, which tallies with the apparent ages of those portrayed.[4]

A. W.

1. It has been suggested that the Mughals appropriated the concept of the royal genealogy from the Ottomans, but there is no solid evidence for this supposition.

2. See Ralph H. Pinder-Wilson, *Paintings from the Muslim Courts of India* (London, 1976), no. 1. There is a considerable number of extant group portraits of Mughal emperors and princes.

3. From left to right, the six sons are: Khalil Mirza, Sayyidi Ahmad Mirza (connected to his son Kichik Mirza), 'Umar Mirza, Suyurghatmish Mirza, Ayyal Mirza, and Abu Bakr Mirza (connected with two sons, Aylankar Mirza and 'Osman Mirza). A vertical line directly below Miran Shah presumably led to the rest of the genealogy from which this portion was taken.

Stylistically, this earlier genealogy resembles one in the Staatliche Museen, Berlin (reproduced in Ernst Kühnel, *Indische Miniaturen aus dem Besitz des Staatlichen Museum zu Berlin* [Berlin, 1941]).

4. The painting of Jahangir and his descendants bears no artist's name. Abu'l-Hasan was well known as a masterly painter of small children (see Stuart C. Welch, *The Art of Mughal*

*India* [New York, 1963], but several of the young princes here do not seem to be by his hand. An attribution to Bichitr, known for his formal portraits, can be tentatively suggested.

PUBLISHED: Ivan Stchoukine, "Portraits moghols, IV: La Collection du Baron Maurice de Rothschild," *Revue des arts asiatiques* 9 (1930): pp. 192–97, no. 1, and fig. 1; Asok Das, *Mughal Painting during Jahangir's Time* (Calcutta, 1978), pp. 139–40 and pl. 33.

## 71 / Shah Jahan and Jahangir
By Balchand and Abu'l-Hasan
India; 1628
Page: H. 55.2 cm., W. 34.5 cm.
Miniature of Shah Jahan (including margins): H. 18.6 cm., W. 14.5 cm.
Miniature of Jahangir (including margins): H. 5.7 cm., W. 4.8 cm.

On a large album page illuminated with repeated floral patterns in light gold, two royal portraits have been mounted. The two portraits were not originally intended for juxtaposition: probably the page was assembled in the eighteenth century. The small size of Jahangir's square portrait and the oval shape of Shah Jahan's derive from English miniature portraits, brought first to Jahangir's attention by Sir Thomas Roe, ambassador from King James I, in 1615. It became fashionable, as well as obviously politic, for a Mughal grandee to wear a small square or oval "jewel" portrait of the emperor.

The sensitive portrait of Jahangir depicts him in the last years of his reign. Balchand, whose name appears on Jahangir's left shoulder, was one of the finest Mughal portraitists, particularly gifted at conveying character and emotions. Thus, despite the radiant aura (the black within it more intense than the black outside) and the strands of perfect pearls (their pigment raised above the paper surface), the focus is on Jahangir as a human being who has learned wisdom and suffered disappointment. One senses too that Balchand found the emperor a sympathetic portrait subject.[1]

The aura around Shah Jahan does not noticeably alter the pale green background, and the sense of volume in the father's portrait has been reduced to flatness in the son's. Clothing, gold, and jewels are more lavish: the figure projects opulent display instead of depth of character, and the outline of the face is knife-sharp, hard, and cold. This portraitist seems to have observed the younger emperor keenly and disliked what he saw. Four inscriptions on the painting of Shah Jahan provide vital information:

1 On the seal that the emperor holds (its writing, of course, should be mirror-image, but for our convenience it has been written normally): "Abu'l-Muzaffar Muhammad Shihab al-Din Shah Jahan Padshah Ghazi, Second Lord of the (auspicious) Astral Conjunction, (in the) year one."[2]

It is an accession seal, marking the first year of the new emperor's reign after several years of princely rebellion against his father, and Shah Jahan regards it with calculating satisfaction.

2 In the upper right: "Written in the first year of the fortunate ascension."

3 In the lower right: "Presented to the sight of the most pure."

4 "The work of the humblest of the servants, Nadir al-Zaman."

From this succinct, precise account it is certain that Abu'l-Hasan, called Nadir al-Zaman, completed the portrait during the first year of the new emperor's reign and presented it to him then for his approval.[3]

Abu'l-Hasan had been Jahangir's favorite painter,[4] and it seems plausible that he should have resented Shah Jahan, who inherited the imperial atelier after many years of fighting his father. A controlled dislike of his new patron may account for this portrait's chilly brilliance, so unlike the warmth and vitality of his other works.

On the reverse is a calligraphic panel containing four lines of *nasta'liq*, probably rendering some of Jami's verses, and signed by Akbar's celebrated scribe Muhammad Husayn.[5]

A. W.

1. For the painter Balchand, see the recent discussion by Milo C. Beach, *The Grand Mogul* (Williamstown, Mass., 1978), pp. 95–101.

2. The title "Second Lord of the Astral Conjunction" explicitly refers to Shah Jahan's valued and much vaunted ancestor, Timur, who styled himself "First Lord of the Astral Conjunction" (see Anthony Welch, *Calligraphy in the Arts of the Muslim World* [Austin and London, 1979], no. 82).

3. Shah Jahan was thirty-six years old at the time.

4. Jahangir records in his *Memoirs* the following comments on Abu'l-Hasan's accession portrait for him: "On this day Abu'l-Hasan, the painter, who has been honored with the title Nadir al-Zaman, drew the picture of my accession as the frontispiece to the *Jahangirnamah*, and brought it to me. As it was worthy of all praise, he received endless favors. His work was perfect, and his picture was one of the chefs d'oeuvre of the age. At the present time he has no rival or equal" (*Tuzuk-i Jahangiri*, trans. A. Rogers, ed. H. Beveridge [London, 1909–1914], p. 20).

5. See cat. nos. 57 and 69 for other works by Muhammad Husayn and further information about him.

PUBLISHED: Beach, *Grand Mogul*, pp. 92, 101.

## 72 / Tulips and an Iris

Attrib. to the Master of the Borders
India; ca. 1645–1650
Page: H. 32 cm., W. 20.2 cm.
Miniature: H. 26.4 cm., W. 16.1 cm.

This is a picture startling in its simplicity and stirring in its richness. The yellow-tan paper supplies no sky, provides distant background, and sup-

**72** / (also in color)

ports only a meager, slightly rising line of moss at the bottom of the page. Towering over this minute landscape is a colossus, a common tulip far too vital and too large for the ground in which it seems to grow. Its erect stalk undulates slightly, and its single leaf of rich and subtly variegated green curves about the stalk and inclines its tip as if in a slow and measured dance around a center. The blossom is in full and perfect bloom: the shades of pink and streaks of yellow rich and luminous, the petals crisply curving and just open enough to reveal the depth of pink along their inner surfaces. The iris, to the right and farther back, is less splendidly dramatic and varicolored, but it is painted with marvelous subtlety, the cupped petals slightly parted to reveal pollen like the softest powder. To the left and seemingly far in the distance, a Western Asiatic tulip (indigenous to Kashmir but not to the rest of India) appears more modest still, with gently drooping leaves and bent head.

This personified analysis is appropriate, for these are highly individual portraits. Other Mughal painters have been keenly observant, but the unnamed master here was more ambitious, bent on capturing the essence of each flower—its tulipness, its irisness. Thus, despite the technical illogic of their setting, they "live" and dominate their environment, which is far vaster than it seems initially, for through a combination of decreasing size and increasing simplicity the iris and the second tulip recede to a great depth. In its very simplicity this recession is a remarkable artistic achievement, transcending the linear and atmospheric perspectives adopted from European art by Mughal painters more than fifty years before.[1]

Mughal patrons had long been fascinated by flowers. Babur's *Memoirs* contain his frequent detailed observations on the flowers and vegetation of the lands he passed through. Jahangir too was a keen observer, distinguishing the individual from the general, noting the real while making obeisance to the ideal, and recording (both in his *Memoirs* and in the art that he commissioned) what struck him as new, exotic, and different. European herbals began to be studied by Mughal artists during his reign,[2] and artists like Manohar and Mansur made flower studies based upon them. In their stark solitude and simplicity, however, the two tulips and iris here are closer to the jewel-and-stone flowers in the walls of the Taj Mahal than they are to other Mughal floral studies. It may well be that the master responsible for this painting had, like Farrukh Beg and Muhammad 'Ali,[3] either come from or spent part of his career in the Deccan. It is also highly probable that he is the anonymous Master of the Borders who created the superb decorated margins for Shah Jahan's albums.[4] *Tulips and an Iris* is the only independent painting that can as yet be attributed to this remarkable artist. That he was principally an illuminator may explain his anonymity. It may also explain his strength, for in an area of art often considered secondary he produced great painting and transformed humble decoration into creativity of a high order.[5]

On the reverse are seven seal impressions and accompanying inscriptions which state that this picture was presented to Shah Jahan on three specific occasions: 28 Rabiʿ al-Awwal [in regnal year] 25 (A.D. 1651), 18 Jumada al-Ula 28 (A.D. 1654), and 4 Rajab 29 (A.D. 1655).[6] The inscriptions indicate that Shah Jahan admired the picture and that, in keeping with his well-developed penchant for administrative regularity and sound record-keeping, there was a definite "royal viewing" procedure.

A. W.

1. For examples, see Ivan Stchoukine, *La Peinture indienne* (Paris, 1929), pl. 46.
2. See Robert Skelton, "A Decorative Motif in Mughal Art," in *Aspects of Indian Art*, ed. Pratapaditya Pal (Leiden, 1972), pp. 147–52.
3. See cat. no. 65. For the attribution of this painting and the borders, as well as the title "Master of the Borders," I am grateful to Stuart C. Welch, who also provided much of the argument.
4. See cat. nos. 56, 57, 62, 65, 73, where his work as an illuminator is analyzed in depth.
5. Tulips are a frequent metaphor in Iranian and Turkish mystical and love poetry, and it is clear that floral motifs, whether in decorated margins, architecture, painting, textiles, or ceramics, had wider cultural meanings.
6. I am indebted to Annemarie Schimmel for her identification of these seals.

## 73 / A Love Poem

By Mir ʿAli
India; ca. 1635–1640
Page: H. 37.8 cm., W. 25.6 cm.
Calligraphy: H. 18.2 cm., W. 10 cm.

According to the inscriptions in the upper right and lower left corners, the four diagonal lines of excellent *nastaʿliq* record a poem composed by ʿAli al-Katib and copied here by him. The quality of the script far exceeds the quality of the poem:

> A delightful young man robbed my soul through his coquetry,
> And he devastated my completely ruined heart.
> I have such pain that I cannot describe it to anyone.
> My condition is such that I cannot explain it.

The holograph is presumably the work of Mir ʿAli al-Haravi, who flourished in Herat and Bukhara under Timurid, Safavid, and Uzbek patrons until his death about 1544. His *nastaʿliq* was much admired by the Mughals, who collected samples of his art and also commissioned copies by their own scribes.[1] They must have noted as well that Mir ʿAli had once written a poem in praise of the first Mughal emperor, Babur: the scribe appears to have been interested in joining the migration of talent to India. Abuʾl-Fazl shared the prevailing Mughal attitude toward the master:

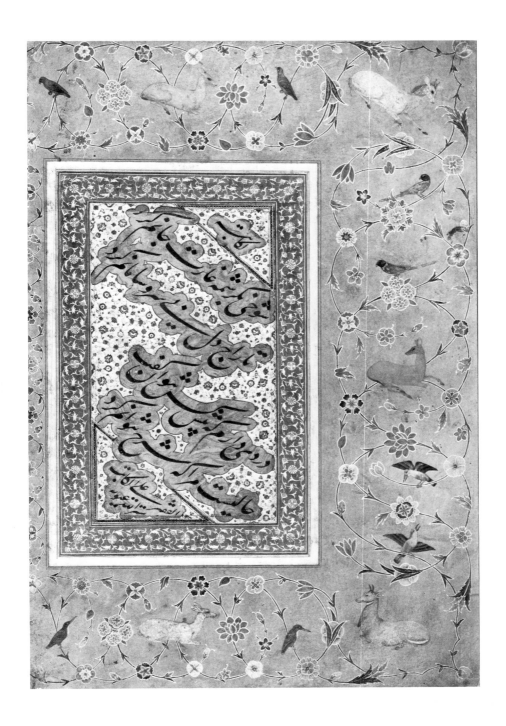

**73** / (also in color)

"[The illustrious Mawlana Mir 'Ali] . . . brought his art to perfection by imitating the writing of Sultan 'Ali of Mashhad. The new method, which he established, is a proof of his genius; he has left many masterpieces."[2]

And Abu'l-Fazl's Iranian contemporary, the Safavid official and chronicler Qadi Ahmad, not only accorded him the highest praise but added that "albums, specimens, and writings of the Mir are scattered throughout the inhabited quarter of the world."[3]

This page once belonged to one of the several great albums commissioned by Shah Jahan; originally calligraphies alternated with figural paintings, all arranged so that they formed a harmonious aesthetic entity. The visual cohesion of these albums must have depended as much upon the pages' illuminated borders as upon their relationship one to another. The decorated margin here is clearly the work of the Master of the Borders, who was responsible for the marginal decorations of several other works in this exhibition.[4] The distinctive elements of his style are clear: individual petals, leaves, and stems are bordered with shining gold, like jewels in a precious setting (this illuminator's art must have stirred the lapidary passions of the emperor!); an arabesque that seems to swirl with utter natural ease obeys instead a strict geometry and moves with principled precision; deer rest at measured intervals, and some birds perch attentively while others poise about to land or fly. It is a world closely observed in all its natural details but set in an order too obvious and too exact for nature: the world as it should be rather than the world as it is.

It was this kind of visual idealism that so appealed to Shah Jahan and so differentiated him from Jahangir and Akbar. Deer and birds are balanced here in a perfect equilibrium of color, shape, and arabesque, and the margins act as lyrical complement to the measured rhythms of the script. Illuminated borders rank among the highest and most sophisticated works of art created under the emperor's aegis, and though a follower of the Master of the Borders (presumably his student) produced impressive work that entered imperial albums,[5] it was the Master of the Borders who combined the utmost skill with perfect artistic manners: his work is unobtrusive brilliance, not begging to be noticed but, once seen, demanding scrutiny. It is this kind of decoration, on the face of it humble and subservient to figural painting or calligraphy (or architecture, as in the Taj Mahal), that is ultimately the key to comprehending Shah Jahan's aesthetics.

A. W.

1. For a brief discussion of Mir 'Ali, see Anthony Welch, *Calligraphy in the Arts of the Muslim World* (Austin and London, 1979), no. 83 and pp. 191–92. I am indebted to Annemarie Schimmel for the above translation.

2. Abu'l-Fazl, *A'in-i Akbari*, trans. H. Blochmann (Calcutta, 1927), 1:108.

3. Qadi Ahmad, *Calligraphers and Painters*, trans. Vladimir Minorsky (Washington, D.C., 1959), p. 131.

4. See cat. nos. 56 (reverse), 57 (obverse and reverse), 62 (reverse), 75 (obverse and reverse). A page in the Los Angeles County Museum of Art (reproduced in Milo C. Beach, *The Grand Mogul* [Williamstown, Mass., 1978], cpl. 23) closely resembles cat. no. 73: though the signature is incomplete, the calligraphy is unquestionably by Mir 'Ali, and the two works may have been on facing pages in the same album. A portrait of Shah Jahan on the Peacock Throne in a private collection has margins also decorated by the Master of the Borders (reproduced in Basil W. Robinson et al., *Persian and Mughal Art* [London, 1976], no. 95.)

5. For margins by a follower of the Master of the Borders, see cat. nos. 56 (obverse) and 62 (obverse). For another page of calligraphy by Mir 'Ali in Prince Sadruddin's collection, see Anthony Welch, *Calligraphy in the Arts of the Muslim World* (Austin and London, 1979), no. 83.

## 74 / Akbar in Old Age

India; ca. 1645
Page: H. 36.8 cm., W. 25.4 cm.
Miniature: H. 21.6 cm., W. 12.7 cm.

Akbar was long dead when this portrait was painted, and it portrays him not as he would have wished to be seen but as his grandson Shah Jahan wanted to remember him. Akbar died in 1605 at the age of sixty-four, and shortly before his death he had commissioned Basawan's son Manohar to paint a group portrait showing the emperor, a courtier, a hunter, and the princes Khusrau and Khurram (the future Shah Jahan).[1] There Akbar is shown pale and exhausted, simply dressed and provided with few of the trappings of power.

The future Shah Jahan, then about twelve years old, was extremely fond of his grandfather, and he remained with him during his dying hours. When this posthumous portrait of Akbar was painted, Shah Jahan himself was in his mid-fifties and may have felt especial empathy for the aged Akbar he had known. In fact, Akbar seems here to be stretching out his hand in welcome to his grandson. But except for this human touch and the accurate likeness of Akbar, it could be any one of the formal imperial portraits to which Shah Jahan was so much addicted. Akbar stands not on a hillock but on the world orb, a common conceit in portraits of Shah Jahan (whose regnal name means Emperor of the World), though the flowers and the insects on some of them (a result of the influence derived from Dutch art) lend a gentler, natural note to the symbol. There is little sense of volume or weight in the figure, whose hand barely rests on his sword, and this kind of flat, weightless immobility is again one of the chief characteristics of Shah Jahan's art. The margins are replete with the equipage of formalized grandeur. Three royal servitors at the left bear a shield, a sword, and a royal parasol, while two *putti* (derived from European prints) hold a protective canopy over the departed emperor and symbolize divine benediction on the Mughal royal house. A posthumous portrait has been turned into an image of the state, and vibrant life has been replaced by

74

calculated references. What we see here is Shah Jahan's temperament expressed in Akbar's form.

This portrait was originally bound in the *Late Shah Jahan Album*, compiled for the emperor in the last decade of his reign.[2]

A. W.

1. Cincinnati Art Museum, no. 1950.289 (see Stuart C. Welch, *Imperial Mughal Painting* [New York, 1978], pl. 15; Milo C. Beach, *The Grand Mogul* [Williamstown, Mass., 1978], fig. 11).

2. Beach, *Grand Mogul*, pp. 76–77. The album was apparently dispersed in 1909. Our analysis of this portrait owes much to the article by Stuart C. Welch cited below.

PUBLISHED: Percy Brown, *Indian Painting under the Mughals* (Oxford, 1924), pl. 26; Stuart C. Welch, "Mughal and Deccani Miniature Paintings from a Private Collection," *Arts Orientalis*, vol. 5 (1963), fig. 17.

## 75 / A Floral Fantasy

India; ca. 1650
Page: H. 23.5 cm., W. 16.1 cm.
Miniature: H. 20.5 cm., W. 13.1 cm.

Nature is shown at full perfection in this painting: roses, plum blossoms, violets, and irises are either buds about to open or blossoms in full bloom, and the undulating hillside is swathed in several shades of green. A tiny stream in the lower right waters this lushness, and shell-like clouds in the sunny sky promise rain. Sky merges with landscape behind the hill. Two butterflies, a lady-bug, and a bee fly toward the blossoms, and two doves on the plum branch complete this miniature paradise. The exuberance of this "garden" is almost overdone: by their disproportionate size the enormous roses at the peak of perfection transform it into a lush, romantic vision.

Floral paintings from Safavid Iran are generally more formal and more decorative; Mughal flowers are usually more naturalistic and exacting in their detail, tending toward description rather than romance. This picture was painted in the Deccan, in central India, almost certainly at the Muslim court of Golconda, a Shi'a kingdom and the diamond emporium of India. Golconda supported a vibrant cultural life, attracting artists, scholars, merchants, and travellers from all over the Muslim world. Traditionally Golconda sustained strong cultural ties with Shi'a Safavid Iran, but in 1687 its Qutb-Shahi dynasty succumbed to Mughal forces, and it became part of Awrangzeb's expanded and short-lived empire.

Neither patron nor artist is identified on this painting, and there is no information on its reverse. But like Golconda itself, it is distinctive and cosmopolitan. The larger blossoms recall Safavid floral paintings like those

75 / (also in color)

226

of Muhammad Zaman,[1] whose work may have been known in the Deccan, and the almost overwhelming size of the roses recalls the large scale of the tulip in catalogue number 72. The resemblance between the irises in the two paintings is even closer and supports the surmise that the painter of the Mughal *Tulips and an Iris* may have spent time in the Deccan. But Western prints exerted an influence too: not only is the subject matter based ultimately on European herbals, but the alighting insects are derived from the Dutch, and the soft "spotting" technique in the grassy ground is clearly a translation of print technique. Despite the major influences from Iran, the Mughal empire, and Europe, the painting remains the product of a different sort of vision, less decorative than the Safavid, less naturalistic than the Mughal, less factual and less moralizing than the Dutch.

A. W.

1. See Ernst Grube, *Islamic Paintings from the 11th to the 18th Century in the Collection of Hans P. Kraus* (New York, 1972), pl. 39. Basil W. Robinson et al., *Persian and Mughal Art* (London, 1976), nos. 62–65, reproduces floral studies by other, later Iranian masters.

## 76 / Woman in a Landscape

India, Deccan; ca. 1670
Page: H. 24.8 cm., W. 22.3 cm.
Miniature: H. 12 cm., W. 5.7 cm.

The Muslim kingdoms of the Deccan sustained strong cultural ties with Safavid Iran over many years, and a number of Iranian artists traveled to Deccani courts in search of patronage. Among them was the Iranian painter Shaykh 'Abbasi, whose most notable Safavid works date to the 1660s and 1670s.[1] His Deccani years gave him material for miniatures done in Isfahan that depict Indian subjects,[2] and he was the natural choice to record for the Safavid shah 'Abbas II the visit of an ambassador from the Mughal court in 1663–1664.[3] His impact on Deccani painting seems to have been considerable.

This miniature also appears to be the work of a master who later returned to Iran. It bears the name Bahram Sufrakash: the last name, meaning "he who spreads out the tablecloth," presumably refers either to the family profession or to the official sinecure that he held. It is dated to 1640–1641 (A.H. 1050). The painter's name is otherwise unknown, and on stylistic grounds the date seems about thirty years too early.

Indianizing works done for the Safavids show unmistakable Iranian traits, particularly in the landscape. But the foliage and the distant village in this painting are found in many Deccani pictures and do not conform to known Iranian taste. In these respects the picture differs from a second miniature, roughly contemporary, that shows the same female type, if not

228

the same woman, and that is almost certainly by the same artist, although it is unsigned. Despite an Indian hermit's cave in the background, the landscape rocks and vegetation in this second miniature are Iranian, and the work was completed after the artist returned from India.[4]

A. W.

1. Robert Skelton has analyzed this painter's work and career in depth.
2. See Basil W. Robinson et al., *Islamic Painting and the Arts of the Book: The Keir Collection* (London, 1976), no. III.395.
3. See Anthony Welch, *Shah 'Abbas and the Arts of Isfahan* (New York, 1973), no. 62.
4. See Basil W. Robinson et al., *Persian and Mughal Art* (London, 1976), no. 59.

## 77 / A Sea Serpent Swallows the Royal Fleet
India; ca. 1670–1686
Page: H. 39 cm., W. 23.5 cm.
Miniature: H. 26.8 cm., W. 14.3 cm.

The Deccani city of Bijapur had been taken by Muslim forces in 1294, but it was not until 1489 that it emerged as a separate Shi'a Muslim kingdom under the 'Adil-Shahi dynasty, whose rule lasted until 1686, when Bijapur was annexed to Awrangzeb's Mughal empire. The 'Adil-Shahis were expansive patrons of architecture, literature, and painting and made their court at Bijapur a major center of Islamic culture and a magnet for talent from all over the Muslim world.

This page originally belonged to a copy of a heroic epic, written in impressive Deccani Urdu by an unknown author who, according to the colophon, "lived during the reign of 'Ali 'Adil Shahi, under whom [he] grew prosperous."[1] Although there were two Bijapur sultans by this name, the very high quality Deccani *naskh* and the painting style indicate that the reference could only be to 'Ali II ibn Muhammad 'Adil Shahi, who ruled from 1656 to 1672. This copy of the epic was probably produced near the end of his reign or during the reign of his successor, Sikandar 'Ali Shah (1672–1686). There is no citation of a patron, royal or otherwise, and this fine manuscript might well have been completed for a prominent aristocrat.

The sea has been transformed into a scene of horror. Turtles, giant crabs, feathery-finned fish of all sizes, and demon-headed phantasmagoria pack the water, and in the upper right a merman and a mermaid paddle unperturbed toward a blank-eyed but very toothy fish. The giant serpent itself is a marvelous creation, revealing the painter's talent and fine training. Water flows like a silvery veil over some of the monster's golden scales, and his body is coiled into a perfect oval that traps the fleet of six ships. The artist was evidently not a sailor, and his sailing vessels have been loosely

adapted from European representations. Human reactions are varied: some of the crew are fighting the serpent with axes, bows, and guns, but most of the passengers only lift their hands in prayers for deliverance. Pricked lightly by arrows, the monster contentedly cracks a boat between his teeth.

On the reverse are four lines of text in two columns.

A. W.

1. Quoted in Christie's catalogue, *Important Islamic and Indian Manuscripts and Miniatures*, London, 10 October 1979, lot 185. There is an excellent discussion of this manuscript, as well as an extensive bibliography, in this entry.

## 78 / A Late Mughal Outing

India, Delhi; ca. 1730–1738
Page: H. 30.7 cm., W. 46.2 cm.
Miniature: H. 19.3 cm., W. 30.3 cm.

The deep blue river recedes between groves of shade trees to distant, bluish mountains. In the middle ground sit four women, enjoying the shade and conversation: the group conforms to similar compositions in many late Mughal paintings. But the six closer women do not; they are strongly influenced, as is the landscape setting itself, by European prints.[1] In the branches at the lower left is inconspicuously written the name Mahmud, perhaps the painter.

Stylistically, the picture belongs to the reign of Muhammad Shah (1719–1748), who gave up his initial efforts to restore the declining Mughal empire in favor of self-indulgence, thus earning the nickname "Pleasure Lover." He was an enthusiastic patron of music, dancing, and painting,[2] but he presided over one of the worst calamities to strike the empire. In 1738–1739 Nadir Shah (r. 1736–1749), who had first aided and then supplanted the Safavid shahs of Iran, invaded northern India and seized and sacked Delhi. His loot included not only the Mughals' Peacock Throne but also some notable treasures from the Imperial Library. This painting must have been among them, for its margins—brilliant gold illuminated with a rich profusion of roses, irises, and smaller flowers—indicate that it was once mounted in a nineteenth-century Qajar album, many of whose borders were decorated by Muhammad Sadiq. In the lower center of this painting's border is an inscription in faint red that appears to read "the humblest Muhammad Baqir."[3]

On the reverse are three panels of calligraphy. Two are examples of *mashq* (calligraphic exercise) that were fine enough to preserve. The upper-

78 /

most text is a prayer signed by ʿImad al-Husayni (Mir ʿImad), one of the most celebrated Safavid calligraphers.[4]

A. W.

1. The three foreground figures reappear in almost identical form in a drawing in the Musée Guimet, Paris (see Stuart C. Welch, *The Art of Mughal India* [New York, 1963], pl. 79). Presumably the Paris drawing is based on this painting, or the two derive from the same European print. The drawing appears to be slightly later in date than the painting.

2. For Muhammad Shah and his patronage, see Welch, *Art of Mughal India*, pp. 141–42 and pls. 77–79; and idem, *Imperial Mughal Painting* (New York, 1978), pl. 39.

3. Muhammad Baqir was known for his floral studies. For an early-nineteenth-century example, see Basil W. Robinson et al., *Persian and Mughal Art* (London, 1976), no. 65 xxiii.

4. For Mir ʿImad, see Anthony Welch, *Shah ʿAbbas and the Arts of Isfahan* (New York, 1973), no. 16; and idem, *Calligraphy in the Arts of the Muslim World* (Austin and London, 1979), no. 56. We are grateful to Annemarie Schimmel for examining and identifying these texts.

## 79 / Colonel Polier's *Nautch*
By Mihr Chand
India, Oudh, Lucknow, or Faizabad; ca. 1780
Page: H. 28.7 cm., W. 39.1 cm.
Miniature: H. 18.9 cm., W. 28.1 cm.

Antoine Louis Henri Polier (1741–1795) left his native Switzerland when he was sixteen years old to serve in the British East India Company as a military engineer. Dissatisfied with the Company, in 1772 he joined the service of Shujaʿ al-Daulat, the ambitious Nawab of Oudh, a wealthy and powerful state that inherited some of the status and authority of the Mughal empire in decline. Polier grew quickly rich and assumed many of the roles of a cultured Indian prince: he became a patron of musicians, poets, and painters; collected calligraphies, paintings, and manuscripts; and compiled at least one impressive *muraqqaʿ* (album). He also sustained lavish entertainments, one of which is recorded here by Mihr Chand, perhaps the foremost Lucknow painter. Other Europeans also came to Oudh to share in its wealth and luxury, until the *nawabs* were completely supplanted by the British during the reign of Asaf al-Daulat. Polier returned to Europe, married, and was murdered by robbers in 1795.

Off-white gowns, lamps, walls, and terrace accentuate otherwise brilliant color: a gaudy yellow couch, the red and green canopy, the musicians' turbans and the dancers' dresses, and swirls and bursts of red and gold in the background fireworks display. Smoking a hookah while he fixedly watches the *nautch* (dance), Colonel Polier assumes a pose favored by other Europeans who pictured themselves as Indian princes.[1] Humbly written on the floor beneath the couch is the painter's name in Persian: "Mihr Chand, son of Gunga Ram." Mughal-trained and European-influenced,

**79** / (also in color)

Mihr Chand was the most significant Indian painter in late eighteenth-century Oudh and was known for his fine copies of European portraits as well as for his sensitive original compositions. Shujaʿ al-Daulat moved his capital from Lucknow to Faizabad in 1765: a dated painting by the English artist Tilly Kettle shows Polier in Faizabad in 1772,[3] and a group portrait by Johann Zoffany shows Polier and other Oudh Europeans in Lucknow in 1786 or 1787.[4] This portrait, of about 1780, might have been painted in either city.

Almost certainly this portrait of Polier as patron was the first folio of an album compiled by the Swiss engineer. On the other side is an illuminated *shamsa* (sunburst), the standard opening image for a fine album.[5] Provided with Europeanizing borders, the *muraqqaʿ* contained the traditional combination of images and calligraphies, one of which is dated to 1781 (A.H. 1195).[6] Apparently before leaving India in 1789, Polier gave the album to Lady Coote, the widow of Sir Eyre Coote (1726–1783), an officer in the British East India Company who had been notable in the military struggles against the French in India.

A. W.

1. See Stuart C. Welch, *Room for Wonder: Indian Painting during the British Period, 1760–1820* (New York, 1978), nos. 36, 37, 46, 53.

2. Ibid., no. 35, a portrait of the Nawab Shujaʿ al-Daulat, copied from an original oil by the English artist Tilly Kettle, who came to Faizabad in 1772. The copy was originally included in the Polier album. Before joining the service of Shujaʿ al-Daulat, Mihr Chand had worked for the Mughal emperor Shah ʿAlam II (first reign, 1760–1788), whose portrait he had painted.

3. Ibid., no. 36.

4. See Mildred Archer, *India and British Portraiture, 1770–1825* (London, 1979). Included in the group are Claud Martin and John Wombwell.

5. The *shamsa* here is very similar to a *shamsa* in Regina Hickmann and Volkmar Enderlein, *Indische Albumblätter, Miniaturen und Kalligraphen aus der Zeit der Moghul-Kaiser* (Leipzig and Weimar, 1979), pl. 60. This second *shamsa* was also made for Polier.

6. See Edwin Binney, 3rd, *Persian and Indian Miniatures from the Collection of Edwin Binney, 3rd* (Portland, Ore., 1973), no. 113; and Anthony Welch, *Calligraphy in the Arts of the Muslim World* (Austin and London, 1979), no. 87.

PUBLISHED: Welch, *Room for Wonder*, no. 34.

## 80 / Story-teller, Dancer, and Musicians

India, Delhi; ca. 1810–1820
Page: H. 30.5 cm., W. 41.6 cm.
Miniature: H. 29.4 cm., W. 40.7 cm.

A number of British patrons of Indian painting were fascinated not only by India's flora and fauna but also by its natural topography, its indigenous architecture, and its social customs. Storytelling and music-making of the sort shown here were vital parts of Indian culture, and the unidentified

artist who painted this scene offers a keen impression of its drama and color. Against a whitewashed wall and under a white canopy nine musicians either clap rhythm or play instruments while a man dances and a youth recites an accompanying tale.[1] The steps of the platform on which they stand are marked by pale blue and pink washes, and similarly pale yellows, oranges, greens, reds, and blues accent the trousers, belts, and turbans of the players. In high Safavid and Mughal art musicians are also frequently shown in performance, but the musical tradition they represent is wholly classical, in keeping with the princely culture of their patrons. What is shown here is no less vital, though on a different level.

This picture was painted for William Fraser, perhaps the most perceptive of all British patrons in India, who guided his artists with Jahangir-like devotion. Following his wishes, they projected an exact, sharp-eyed view of India and its people. In effect, they strove to be cameras at a time well before the invention of photography. At their best, the more sensitive and subtle of Fraser's artists carried the Mughal tradition a step further.

S. C. W. and A. W.

1. This page originally belonged to the Fraser album. English and *nasta'liq* inscriptions on a thin sheet of cover-paper identify the individual performers.

# List of Illustrations

**Library of Congress Cataloging in Publication Data**

Welch, Anthony.
    Arts of the Islamic book.

    "Catalogue of an exhibition organized by the Asia Society . . . presented at the Society's headquarters in New York City and also at the Kimbell Art Museum, Fort Worth, and the Nelson Gallery–Atkins Museum, Kansas City"—Verso t.p.
    1. Illumination of books and manuscripts, Islamic—Exhibitions. 2. Miniature painting, Islamic—Exhibitions. 3. Aga Khan, Sadruddin, Prince, 1933–   —Art collections—Exhibitions. I. Welch, Stuart Cary. II. Asia Society. III. Kimbell Art Museum, Fort Worth. IV. William Rockhill Nelson Gallery of Art and Mary Atkins Museum of Fine Arts, Kansas City, Mo. V. Title.
ND2955.W44   1982   745.6'7'0917671074013   82-71587
ISBN 0-8014-1548-9 (cloth)           AACR2
ISBN 0-8014-9882-1 (pbk.)